Flughafen
Berlin Brandenburg
Willy Brandt
Berlin Brandenburg
Airport Willy Brandt

Meinhard von Gerkan
Hubert Nienhoff
Hans Joachim Paap

Flughafen Berlin Brandenburg Willy Brandt

Berlin Brandenburg Airport Willy Brandt

gmp FOCUS

gmp · Architekten von Gerkan, Marg und Partner

Verortung

Location

52° 21' 44" N, 13° 30' 2" O

Berlin gehörte zu Beginn des 20. Jahrhunderts neben London, Paris und New York zu den dynamischsten Metropolen der Welt, geprägt durch rasantes Wachstum, eine stürmische industrielle Entwicklung und Innovationsgeist – eine Stadt wie geschaffen für die Fliegerei. Kurz nach 1900 entstanden in Berlin Flughäfen sowohl für Flugzeuge als auch für Luftschiffe: der Flugplatz Johannisthal und die Luftschiffwerft in Staaken. So dynamisch sich die Fliegerei vom viel bestaunten Wunderwerk zum Alltagsgeschäft entwickelte, so schnell gewann die Bauaufgabe Flughafen an Bedeutung: Auf Johannisthal und Staaken folgten Tempelhof, Gatow, Tegel und Schönefeld. Keiner der Berliner Flughäfen der ersten Stunde wird heute noch genutzt, von manchen ist kaum noch etwas im Stadtbild zu erkennen.

At the beginning of the 20th century, Berlin–alongside London, Paris, and New York–was one of the most dynamic metropolises in the world. With its rapid growth, fast-paced industrial development, and innovative spirit, the city was destined to open itself up for aviation. Shortly after 1900, Berlin saw the development of airports for aircraft as well as airships: Johannisthal Airport and the airship yard in Staaken. As aviation developed rapidly from marvelled at innovation to day-to-day business, the task of building airports became more and more important: Johannisthal and Staaken were followed by Tempelhof, Gatow, Tegel, and Schönefeld. Today, none of these early airports are still in use; some of them have disappeared almost completely from the cityscape.

Von Schönefeld in die Welt

From Schönefeld into the World

Der Flughafenstandort Schönefeld liegt außerhalb der Berliner Stadtgrenze. Seine Ursprünge gehen auf die Henschel-Flugzeugwerke zurück, die im Rahmen der nationalsozialistischen Aufrüstungspolitik in Schönefeld Flugzeuge herstellten, sowie auf die in unmittelbarer Nachbarschaft gelegene Erprobungsstelle der Luftfahrtindustrie, Diepensee. Deren Gebäude beherbergten 1946, im sowjetischen Sektor gelegen, die erste Abfertigung für Zivilisten in Schönefeld, als die Aeroflot ihren Flugbetrieb von Berlin aus aufnahm. 1955 übergab die Rote Armee den Flughafen an die DDR. 1976 wurde im Norden des Geländes die Neue Passagierabfertigung (NPA), das spätere Terminal L, in Betrieb genommen. Weitergehende Pläne, Schönefeld zu einem Großflughafen auszubauen, wurden nicht verwirklicht – nicht zuletzt, weil das Gelände in unmittelbarer Nähe zur Grenze nach Westberlin lag. Nichtsdestotrotz stieg das Fluggastaufkommen bis 1990 - die DDR-eigene Interflug bediente ab Schönefeld 53 Ziele auf vier Kontinenten. Durch provisorische Ausbauten ergänzt, entwickelte sich der Flughafen nach der Wiedervereinigung zur viel frequentierten Basis von Charterflügen. Mit Inbetriebnahme des Flughafens Berlin Brandenburg (BER) am 31. Oktober 2020 wurde Schönefeld (SXF) als Terminal 5 Teil des BER.

Schönefeld lies outside Berlin's city boundaries. Its origins as an airport go back to the Henschel aircraft works in Schönefeld, which manufactured aircraft as part of the Nazi rearmament policy, and Diepensee, the aviation industry's test facility that is located close by. By 1946 the area belonged to the Soviet-occupied sector, and the buildings at Diepensee were used for handling civilian passengers when Aeroflot started its operations in Berlin. In 1955, the Red Army handed the airport to the German Democratic Republic (GDR). In 1976, operations started at the new passenger handling facility (NPA) in the northern part of the grounds, which later became Terminal L. More ambitious plans to expand Schönefeld into an airport hub were not implemented—not least, because the site was so close to the boundary of what was then West Berlin. Nevertheless, the passenger volume continued to increase until 1990, with the GDR's Interflug Airline operating flights to more than 53 international destinations on four continents, from Schönefeld. After the German reunification, temporary facilities were added and the airport became a popular base for charter flights. With the opening of Berlin Brandenburg Airport (BER) on October 31, 2020, Schönefeld (SXF) became part of the new airport, operating as Terminal 5.

Berlin in Zahlen
Berlin in numbers

Fläche: 891,8 km²
Area: 891.8 km²

Bevölkerung: 3,7 Mio. (2020)
Population: 3.7 million (2020)

1974–2020
⑤ Tegel

1915–53
② Staaken

1935–94
④ Gatow

1923–2008
③ Tempelhof

1909–52/95
① Johannisthal

ab from 2020
Berlin Brandenburg
⑥ Willy Brandt

Berliner Flughäfen/-plätze
Berlin airports/-fields

Schienen
Railway
Wasserwege
Waterways

Mit Stil und Struktur

Engelbert Lütke Daldrup

Berlin hat eine bewegte Luftfahrtgeschichte. Alles begann 1909 mit dem Flugplatz Berlin-Johannisthal. Insbesondere die Luftbrücke der Westalliierten nach der Blockade durch die sowjetische Besatzung in den Jahren 1948/49 hat die Geschichte der Stadt geprägt. Die drei Berliner Flughäfen Tempelhof, Tegel und Gatow standen damals für Freiheit, für die Möglichkeit, sich frei zu bewegen und zu reisen. Und obwohl die DDR-Bürger in der Regel nicht frei reisen konnten, verkörperte der Flughafen Schönefeld doch auch die Sehnsucht nach dieser Freiheit.

Die Flughäfen Johannisthal, Gatow und Tempelhof sind schon lange stillgelegt. Am 8. November 2020 startete mit einer Air-France-Maschine das letzte Flugzeug von Tegel. Der ehemalige Flughafen Schönefeld ist Teil des BER geworden.

Mit dem Flughafen Berlin Brandenburg Willy Brandt (IATA-Code: BER) hat jetzt ganz Berlin, hat der Osten Deutschlands ein gemeinsames Tor zur Welt. Der neue Hauptstadtflughafen im Brandenburgischen ist zudem ein Zeichen für das Zusammenwachsen in der Region.

Die international renommierten Architekten von Gerkan, Marg und Partner (gmp) haben vor mehr als fünfzig Jahren bereits den Flughafen Tegel entworfen. Jahrzehnte später stehen sie auch für den BER. Vor den Toren Berlins haben sie ein Kleinod klassischer Architektur geschaffen: Es vereint Großzügigkeit und Weite mit durchdachter Funktionalität bis ins Detail. Es verbindet Sachlichkeit und Schlichtheit mit Stil und Eleganz.

Schon bei der ersten Annäherung mit dem Flugzeug aus der Luft oder mit dem Auto von der Straße kommend, offenbart der neue Flughafen seinen Gästen, was ihn ausmacht: Es ist neben der Dimension des 1470 Hektar großen Areals vor allem die eindrucksvolle Klarheit der räumlichen und funktionalen Struktur.

Allein die 32 Meter hohe Abfertigungshalle mit ihrer gläsernen Front von 220 Metern Länge erzeugt ein luftiges Ambiente. Filigrane Stützen rhythmisieren die Abflughalle und tragen die transluzente Membran des Daches. Unter dem weit auskragenden Dach haben die Architekten nahezu alles vereint, was Reisende heute brauchen: Check-in und Gepäckaufgabe, Sicherheitskontrolle, Einkaufsmeile, Gastronomie und Gepäckausgabe. Logisch angeordnet, komfortabel und konzipiert für gewaltige Menschenströme. Materialien wie dunkler Nussbaum an Countern und Wänden und Millionen Jahre alter Kalksandstein am Boden vermitteln dazu Behaglichkeit.

Hinzu kommt ein Vorzug, wie ihn kein anderer Flughafen in Deutschland hat: Der große Bahnhof direkt unter dem Terminal, an dem bereits heute schon 14 Züge pro Stunde halten und der genügend Platz für neue ICE-Verbindungen und damit eine klimafreundliche Anreise bietet. Passagiere, die dort ankommen, sind in wenigen Minuten am Check-in in der Abflughalle. Ein Luxus der kurzen Wege.

Geradezu spielerisch hebt sich von aller Rationalität der filigrane rote Teppich unter dem Dach der Abflughalle ab – „THE Magic Carpet" der kalifornischen Künstlerin Pae White. Er ist inzwischen zum Markenzeichen des BER avanciert und erzählt auf seine Weise eine Geschichte vom freien Reisen.

Wir alle wissen: Die Geschichte des BER war von vielen Konflikten, Wirrnissen und Fehlschlägen begleitet. Das ist mittlerweile bei derart komplexen Großprojekten leider üblich. Lange wurde zwischen Berlin, Brandenburg und dem Bund gefeilscht, wo der neue Flughafen errichtet werden soll. Letztlich setzte sich 1996 im „Konsensbeschluss" die stadtnahe Anbindung gegen die Lärmschutzinteressen der Nachbarschaft durch. Es dauerte zehn Jahre, bis der Planungsprozess von der Standortentscheidung über den gescheiterten Privatisierungsversuch mit der Entscheidung des obersten deutschen Verwaltungsgerichts abgeschlossen wurde. Mit der rechtskräftigen Planfeststellung wurde im Jahr 2006 Baurecht für den neuen Flughafen für Berlin und Brandenburg geschaffen. Sechs Jahre später, im Jahr 2012, scheiterte die Eröffnung des BER spektakulär. Es sollte noch weitere acht Jahre dauern, bis die Baukatastrophe schließlich in Ordnung kam. Mit verdoppelten Baukosten, in mühsamer Kleinarbeit.

Letztlich wurden alle notwendigen Prüfungen erfolgreich abgeschlossen, die Nutzungsfreigabe der Baubehörden wurde erreicht. Im Frühjahr 2020 war das Terminal 1 als letztes der vierzig Gebäude des BER fertiggestellt. Nach sechsmonatigem Probebetrieb landeten schließlich am 31. Oktober 2020 die ersten Maschinen am neuen Fluggastterminal. An diesem Tag wurde auch den Letzten klar: Der BER ist - endlich - eröffnet.

With Style and Structure

Berlin has an eventful aviation history. Everything started in 1909 with Berlin-Johannisthal Airport. After the war, particularly the airlift organized by the Western Allies in response to the blockade, imposed by the Soviet occupying forces in 1948/49, had a major impact on the history of the city. At that time, the three Berlin airports, Tempelhof, Tegel, and Gatow, were a symbol of freedom, of the possibility to freely move and travel. Although GDR citizens were normally not at liberty to travel, Schönefeld Airport symbolized the longing for this freedom.

The Johannisthal, Gatow, and Tempelhof airports have long been taken out of service. On 8 November 2020, an Air France plane was the last aircraft to take off from Tegel, while the former Schönefeld Airport became a part of BER.

With Berlin Brandenburg Airport Willy Brandt (IATA code BER), all of Berlin, and all of eastern Germany, now has a shared gate to the world. In addition, the German capital's new airport in the Brandenburg region is a symbol of the region growing together.

More than fifty years ago, the internationally renowned architects von Gerkan, Marg and Partners (gmp) designed the former Tegel Airport. Decades later, they also took on the responsibility for designing the new BER Airport. They have created a jewel of classic architecture just outside Berlin: combining generosity and breadth with meticulous attention to functionality and detail. It combines a plain and rational approach with style and sophistication.

Whether approaching the new airport by plane or by car, it is clear what makes it remarkable: covering 1,470 hectares, it stands with impressive clarity in its spatial and functional structure.

The 32-meter-high check-in hall, with its 220-meter-long glass front, generates an airy ambiance. Elegant columns give rhythm to the departure hall and support the translucent membrane of the roof. Under the widely cantilevering roof, the architects have placed nearly everything passengers need these days: check-in and checked baggage counters, security control, shopping area, gastronomy, and baggage claim. All this has been arranged in a logical layout that is convenient and designed for huge numbers of people. Materials such as dark walnut on the counters and walls and million-year-old limestone on the floor convey a sense of comfort. Additionally, there is one aspect which makes this airport unique in Germany: the large railway station directly beneath the terminal. Already today, 14 trains stop here every hour, and it has space for new ICE services, thus ensuring environmentally friendly travel to the airport. Passengers arriving there only need a few minutes to get to the check-in counters in the departure hall. The luxury of short routes.

The intricate red carpet beneath the roof of the departure hall—"THE Magic Carpet" by Californian artist Pae White—is a playful contrast to all the rational architecture and procedures. This artwork has now become the trademark of BER and, in its own way, tells the story of the freedom of travel.

We all know that the history of BER was beset by many conflicts and failures, and much confusion. Unfortunately, this is a common occurrence nowadays with such large, complex projects. There was a long period in which Berlin, Brandenburg, and the Federal Government argued about where to locate the new airport. Ultimately, in 1996, the location close to the city prevailed in the "consensus decision" over the noise protection lobby of the neighborhood. It took ten years for the planning process to be completed, starting with the decision on the location via the failed privatization attempt and ending with the ruling of Germany's Supreme Administrative Court. With the legally binding planning approval in 2006, permission was granted for the construction of the new airport for Berlin and Brandenburg. Six years later, in 2012, the opening of BER failed spectacularly. It would take another eight years until the troubled construction project was put right, at double the building cost and with an enormous amount of painstaking work.

In the end, all necessary final checks were successfully passed, and authorization to open the airport was obtained. In the spring of 2020, Terminal 1 was the last of the forty buildings of BER to be completed. After a six-month trial operation, the first planes landed at the new passenger terminal on October 31, 2020. On this day, it became clear even to the doubters: BER is open—finally.

The story of BER's construction and troubles is not an indication of the failure of German engineering, but rather a symbol of our overregulated construction system. Many large building projects illustrate that planning and building in a democratic society means that numerous obstacles have to be overcome due to an increasing

Die Bau- und Leidensgeschichte des BER steht nicht für das Versagen deutscher Ingenieurskunst, sie ist vielmehr ein Symbol für unser überreguliertes Bauwesen. Viele große Bauprojekte zeigen, dass in einer demokratischen Gesellschaft beim Planen und Bauen wegen einer immer größeren Anzahl an Gesetzen, Regeln und Normen mannigfaltige Hindernisse überwunden werden müssen. In unserem System der sektoralen Optimierung von Einzelaspekten des Bauens geht der Blick für das Ganze leider immer mehr verloren.

Brandschutz, Energieeffizienz, Barrierefreiheit, Sicherheitstechnik und Gebäudeleittechniken bestimmen heute viel mehr das Baugeschehen als die klassischen Tugenden des römischen Architekten Vitruv: Firmitas (Festigkeit), Utilitas (Nützlichkeit) und Venustas (Schönheit). Aus dem harmonischen Dreiklang der vitruvschen Kategorien ist ein eklatantes Ungleichgewicht geworden. Aus der Firmitas hat sich ein Moloch entwickelt: ein nahezu unentwirrbares Knäuel gebäudetechnischer Ausrüstungen. Und die Venustas ist allzu oft zur Selbstgefälligkeit der Designer verkommen.

Die exakte Einhaltung aller Regeln und Normen, wie sie beim BER nach der gescheiterten Eröffnung im Jahr 2012 exerziert wurde, macht solch komplexe Gebäude wie das 360.000 Quadratmeter große Fluggastterminal des BER in Deutschland fast nicht mehr bau- oder sanierbar. Funktion oder Gestaltung werden erstickt von explodierenden Normenwerken.

Der Bau des Flughafens Berlin Brandenburg Willy Brandt gelang gerade noch im Rahmen dessen, was heutzutage möglich ist. Wir alle haben mit großem Kraftaufwand das Projekt zu einem guten Ende gebracht und können jetzt ein Terminal bieten, in dem sich die Menschen wohl- und gut aufgehoben fühlen.

Natürlich haben wir uns gewünscht, dass sich nach der Eröffnung mehr Passagiere von der durchdachten Struktur des BER, von seinem hohen technischen Standard und seinem Charme hätten überzeugen können. Aufgrund der Coronapandemie und der weltweiten Reisebeschränkungen war das leider im ersten Betriebsjahr nicht möglich.

Wir werden den Flughafen weiterentwickeln, selbst wenn es länger dauert als gedacht. Er ist nur Teil einer künftigen Flughafenstadt. Zwischen der Autobahn und dem großen Hauptterminal wird mehr als eine klassische Airport City entstehen – nämlich ein lebendiger Stadtteil, in dem sich die Menschen gern aufhalten werden. Nicht nur an Hotels und Konferenzzentren und Bürogebäude ist gedacht, sondern auch an vielfältige Co-Working-Angebote, an Restaurants, Nahversorgung und Kultur. Der BER wird Impulsgeber für die weitere wirtschaftliche Entwicklung im Osten Deutschlands werden. In seinem Umfeld werden in den nächsten Jahren Tausende neue Arbeitsplätze entstehen. Bis zum Jahr 2035 könnten es bis zu 55.000 Menschen sein, die durch den BER ihren Lebensunterhalt verdienen. Große Unternehmen wie der Elektroautoriese Tesla haben sich bereits in der Nähe angesiedelt, andere werden folgen.

Die Zeit des BER wird kommen. Anders geht es nicht mehr in einer globalisierten Welt. Die schnelle Ausbreitung des Coronavirus hat gezeigt, wie eng die Menschen über alle Kontinente hinweg verbunden sind. Die Pandemie hat mit rasender Geschwindigkeit fast alle Staaten erfasst und vor dieselben Probleme gestellt. Nur global ist diese Krise in den Griff zu bekommen, etwa, wenn weltweit genügend Impfstoff zur Verfügung steht. Keine Wirtschaft kann mehr isoliert und abgeriegelt existieren.

Für ein wirtschaftliches Miteinander, für menschliche Kontakte, für einen erweiterten Horizont im Denken und Fühlen reichen See- und Landwege, Zoom-Konferenzen und digitale „Reisen" nicht aus. Die Menschen sehnen sich nach Freiheit und Weite und Weltoffenheit. Dazu bedarf es eines funktionierenden Flugbetriebs.

Der Flughafen Berlin Brandenburg Willy Brandt, der BER, bietet die besten Voraussetzungen für freies und sicheres Reisen.

number of laws, regulations, and standards. In our system of optimizing individual aspects of construction by sector, the ability to see the whole picture is unfortunately becoming harder and harder.

Today, fire protection, energy efficiency, accessibility, security, and building control systems have a much greater impact on building projects than the classical virtues described by the Roman architect Vitruvius: firmitas (structural integrity), utilitas (usefulness), and venustas (beauty). The harmonious triad of the Vitruvian categories has degenerated into a blatant imbalance. Firmitas has developed into a monstrous task: a nearly inextricable tangle of technical building systems. And venustas has all too often become a case of self-indulgence on the part of designers.

If all the rules and standards that were applied after the failed opening in 2012 were to be complied with, such complex buildings as the 360,000-square-meter passenger terminal of BER in Germany would almost be impossible to build or refurbish. Function and design are suffocated by the exploding number of standards.

The construction of Berlin Brandenburg Airport Willy Brandt was barely possible within the bounds of today's parameters. With a huge effort, all of us have brought the project to a successful end and can now offer a terminal that makes people feel secure and comfortable.

Of course, after the opening, we would have liked more passengers to be convinced by the well thought-out structure and the high technical standard, as well as charm, of BER. Unfortunately, owing to the Coronavirus pandemic and worldwide travel restrictions, this was not possible during the first year of operation.

We will continue to develop the airport, even if it takes longer than planned. It is only one part of a future aerotropolis. Between the motorway and the large main terminal, more than just a classic airport city will be developed—a lively urban district where people like to spend time. This includes not only hotels, conference centers, and office buildings, but also various co-working facilities, restaurants, local services, and culture venues. BER will stimulate continued commercial development in the east of Germany. Thousands of new jobs will be created in this aerotropolis in the years to come. By 2035, 55,000 people could be earning their living at or around BER. Large companies such as Tesla, the giant electric car maker, have already established branches close by, and others will follow.

The time of BER airport will come. There is no other way in this globalized world. The fast spread of the Coronavirus has shown how closely people are connected across all continents. The pandemic has struck almost all countries at breakneck speed and confronted them with the same problems. This crisis can only be overcome when there is enough vaccine for everybody worldwide. No economy can exist in isolation, locked away from others.

For commercial cooperation, for human contact, for broadened horizons in thinking and feeling it is not sufficient to embark on land and sea travel, Zoom conferences, and digital "travel." People long for freedom, for the openness of the world without restrictions. This is not possible without a functioning aviation industry.

Berlin Brandenburg Airport Willy Brandt, BER, offers the best conditions for free and safe travel.

Vorwort

Meinhard von Gerkan

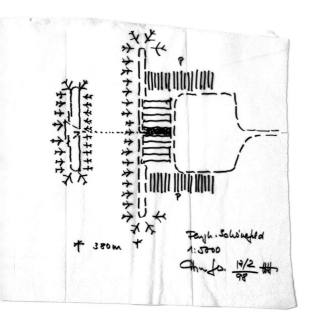

Entwurfsskizze von Meinhard von Gerkan
Design sketch by Meinhard von Gerkan

Mit der Eröffnung des Flughafens Berlin Brandenburg wurde zeitgleich der Flugbetrieb in Berlin-Tegel eingestellt. Oft erzählt ist die Geschichte, wie Volkwin Marg, Klaus Nickels und ich mit diesem Großprojekt unseren Weg als Architekten begannen, ohne dass wir als gerade Diplomierte irgendeine konkrete Berufserfahrung, geschweige denn Referenzen im Flughafenbau nachweisen konnten. Beide Verkehrsbauten trennen rund vier Jahrzehnte, in denen sich fast alle Bedingungen der Bauaufgabe radikal gewandelt haben.

Wenn man die verschiedenen Typologien betrachtet, gibt es die, die einen nahezu dauerhaften Status haben. Ein Theater bleibt immer ein Theater, auch wenn man die Kulissen verschiebt oder die Scheinwerfer elektrisch gesteuert werden und nicht mehr von Hand. Ein Flughafen hingegen ist kein Zustand, sondern ein ewiger Prozess der Veränderung, und zwar immer und überall! Aufgrund der verschiedensten Einflüsse, sei es wegen der Sicherheitskontrollen, des

Flächenbedarfs für den Einzelhandel, wegen immer neuer Abfertigungssysteme, immer größerer Flugzeuge oder neuer Logistiküberlegungen für die Verkehrsverbindungen. In der fortschrittlichsten Verkehrstechnik, dem Fliegen, bilden die Orte des Abfliegens und Ankommens die Achillesferse. Hier werden aus Kapazitätsengpässen Verspätungen erzeugt, hier stößt die Vernetzung mit dem Bodenverkehr auf logistische und städtebauliche Probleme. Deshalb wird jedes unflexible architektonische Konzept in kürzester Zeit obsolet, erfährt radikale Veränderungen und Brüche, wird durch Gegenkonzepte chaotisiert. Es gibt Flughäfen, die kennt man nur als Baustelle. Entweder werden gerade die Decken aufgerissen oder der Fußboden oder beides gleichzeitig. Oder die Wände oder der Weg sind versperrt mit Pappwänden, weil wieder mal eine neue Boutique eingebaut wird.

Wer hätte vor fünfzig Jahren vorausgesehen, dass Verweilflächen wartender Passagiere zu großen Fast-Food-Zonen mit dem bekannten Milieu von Schnellbrateinrichtungen nebst Bratwurst, Pommes-Frites-Bergen und Fettwolken zu Tummelplätzen der Massenfütterung anwachsen und die Flugabfertigung zur nachgeordneten Funktion degradiert wird. Wer hätte geahnt, wie weit sich das flächenfressende Angebot von Weinen, Spirituosen und Umsatzflächen für Luxusartikel ausdehnen würde.

Ein Flughafen muss heute ein offenes System sein, das so wenig Festlegungen und so viel Freiräume wie möglich aufweist, um künftige Veränderungen integrieren zu können. Diese Erkenntnis ist der entscheidende Parameter beim Entwerfen von Flughäfen. Diese müssen im ersten Entwicklungsschritt eine äußerst robuste Struktur besitzen und den übergeordneten Rahmen für Erweiterungsmaßnahmen verbindlich festlegen, dabei jedoch genügend Freiraum lassen für die Vielfalt des Einzelnen. Nur auf diese Weise besteht die Chance, dass ein Gesamtkonzept über viele Jahre gewahrt bleibt und die Logik eines Systems die Oberhand behält, statt sich zu einem funktionalen Irrgarten zu entwickeln. Bei der Planung des neuen Berliner Flughafens hat diese Erkenntnis zu einer radikalen Reduktion aller formalen und gestalterischen Elemente auf das absolut Notwendige und Einfachste geführt: unkompliziert, groß, einfach, schlicht. Wir wollten eine Gesamtfigur entstehen lassen, die architektonisch so stabil und nachhaltig ist, dass sie alle Veränderungen in der Zukunft verkraftet, ohne sich deswegen verwandeln zu müssen oder verschandelt werden zu müssen.

Preface

At the same time as the Berlin Brandenburg Airport was opened, operations at Berlin-Tegel were terminated. The story has often been told of how Volkwin Marg, Klaus Nickels, and I—having just obtained our diplomas—started our careers as architects with this large project, without having any professional experience whatsoever, not to mention any previous experience in the design of airports. The designs of these two aviation hubs are separated by nearly four decades, a time during which almost all design parameters have undergone radical change.

When you consider the various building typologies, there are those that have an almost permanent status. A theater will always remain a theater, even though the backdrops may change, or the footlights may be controlled electronically rather than manually. By comparison, an airport is not set in stone but undergoes a continuous process of change—always and everywhere! This may be due to various factors, be it the security controls, the areas required for retail, the ongoing development of handling systems, ever larger aircraft, or new logistics schemes for the transportation connections. In aviation, the most advanced form of transport, the points of departure and arrival are the Achilles' heel. It is at these points, that delays occur due to capacity restrictions, that logistical and urban design problems arise at the interface with ground traffic. For this reason, any architectural concept that lacks flexibility will become obsolete in a very short time; such airports will be subject to radical changes and reversals—becoming chaotic due to the imposition of alternative concepts. Some airports are known for being permanent construction sites. Either the ceilings are being removed or the floors are being taken up—or both at the same time. Or there are temporary partitions blocking the way because yet another new boutique is being fitted.

Who would have foreseen fifty years ago that departure lounges would become huge fast food zones, places of mass consumption, with the familiar fat-dripping ambiance of catering establishments offering bratwurst, mountains of French fries, etc. and that the actual business of preparing for departure would be degraded to a secondary function? Who could have foreseen to what extent the space required for the retail of wines, spirits, and luxury articles would increase?

Today, an airport has to be an open system, with as few fixed installations and as many open options as possible to enable the integration of future changes. This is the decisive parameter in the design of airports. In the first instance, any new airport must have an extremely robust structure. The design should bindingly define the overall framework for future extensions, while at the same time allowing sufficient space for diversity in the detail. This is the only way to ensure that an overall concept remains intact for many years, and that a system remains operative in accordance with its initial logic rather than developing into a dysfunctional maze. In the design of the new Berlin airport, this understanding has led to a radical reduction of all formal and conceptual elements to what is absolutely necessary and simple: uncomplicated, large, simple, plain. We wanted to create an overall design that is so stable and sustainable in its architecture that it can accommodate all future changes, without having to undergo serious modification or disfiguration.

Hence, the focus in the design of airports must be on the conceptual principle rather than—as is often wrongly assumed—formal design aspects. Both growth and future change are as important as the creation of a functional status quo. My position, which I have always asserted in my teaching of functional planning at university, is that in architecture you should always work down from the large whole to the small detail, rather than the other way around. It would be a big mistake to see architecture as an addition of numerous details that—even though they somehow relate to each other—cannot be forged together into an overall context.

When there is no stringent and dominant overall concept, i.e., the design is "soft," the initial structures are soon abandoned and develop along the principle of day-to-day decisions, creating a wildly sprawling conglomerate, an odd mixture of typologies that do not grow together into a uniform whole, and therefore fail to add any prestige to the place. And yet, this is the fate of almost all the world's airports; this understanding should guide all future airport design.

An equally important parameter in the design of airports is the creation of architectural identity. In the architecture of public buildings in general, the question of proportionality, i.e., the relationship between size and function, and the importance of the building for the city and the people, are of enormous importance—much more so than various details. This is about a lasting effect of how a place is perceived. Therefore, an airport, a modern-day

Das Schwergewicht beim Entwerfen von Flughäfen liegt daher eindeutig im Konzeptionellen und nicht – wie man irrtümlich meinen könnte – im Formal-Gestalterischen. Dabei haben die Parameter Wachstum und Veränderung eine ebenbürtige Bedeutung neben der Schaffung eines funktionsfähigen Status quo. Meine Position, die ich auch als Hochschullehrer immer wieder vertreten habe, ist, dass man in der Architektur etwas immer vom großen Ganzen zum kleinen Ganzen generieren sollte und nicht umgekehrt. Es ist ein großer Fehler, wenn man Architektur als Addition von lauter Einzelheiten versteht, die zwar irgendetwas miteinander zu tun haben, die aber in keinen übergeordneten Zusammenhang gebracht werden können.

Wenn es an einem stringenten und dominanten Gesamtkonzept mangelt, die Konzeption also „weich" ist, werden die begonnenen Strukturen schnell verlassen und entwickeln sich nach dem Prinzip von aktuellen Tagesentscheidungen zu einem wild wuchernden Konglomerat, einem Sammelsurium von Typologien, die nicht zu einer Gemeinsamkeit und einer Einheitlichkeit zusammenwachsen und daher auch nichts Repräsentatives für den Ort haben. Dies ist das Schicksal fast aller Flughäfen der Welt – Flughafenentwürfe sollten sich an dieser Erkenntnis orientieren.

Ein gleichgewichtiger Parameter beim Entwerfen von Flughäfen ist die Schaffung von baulicher Identität. Bei der Architektur öffentlicher Bauten allgemein ist die Frage der Verhältnismäßigkeit, des Verhältnisses von Größe zu dem Bestimmungszweck und der Bedeutung des Gebäudes für die Stadt und die Menschen, von großer Wichtigkeit – viel wichtiger als so manch einzelnes Detail. Da geht es um eine nachhaltige Wirkung der Wahrnehmung eines Ortes. Ein Flughafen, der das neuzeitliche Tor zu einer Stadt darstellt, hat daher geradezu die Verpflichtung, unverwechselbar zu sein und sich als Ort des Ankommens und Abreisens einzuprägen. Diese inhaltsbezogene Identität zu entwickeln, die weder von funktioneller Eingleisigkeit noch von einem gestalterischen Dogma diktiert wird, war uns auch beim Berliner Flughafen ein zentrales Anliegen.

Nicht zuletzt sehe ich in der hinlänglich bekannten und wenig ruhmreichen Planungsgeschichte des Flughafens Berlin Brandenburg, die ich damals für die Zeit, in der wir Verantwortung trugen, in dem Band *Black Box BER* (2013) ausführlich dargelegt habe, eines meiner ältesten Credos bestätigt: Wir brauchen engagierte und kompetente öffentliche Bauherren. Architektur lässt sich nicht aus Gesetzen, Bestimmungen und Erlassen, nicht auf der Basis des Konsumverhaltens oder anderer flüchtiger Modeerscheinungen zusammenschustern. Architektur ist auch nicht nur die Summe von optimalen Teilleistungen vieler Experten und Spezialisten. Architektur ist und bleibt eine geistige und schöpferische Leistung, die in ihrer Ganzheitlichkeit nicht ohne persönliche Verantwortung entstehen kann.

gateway to a city, could be said to have an obligation to be unmistakable and to clearly stand out as a place of arrival and departure. Developing this content-related identity that is neither dictated by functional oversimplification nor by design-related dogma was a key objective in our design for the Berlin airport.

In the well-known and rather troubled design history of Berlin Brandenburg Airport, which I explained in detail in my publication *Black Box BER* (2013) for the time when we were responsible for the project, I see one of my longest held credos confirmed: we need committed and competent persons representing the public client. Architecture cannot be cobbled together on the basis of laws, regulations, and decrees, nor on the basis of consumer behavior or other fleeting fashions. Neither is architecture the sum of perfect individual achievements of experts and specialists. Architecture is and will remain a creative and intellectual achievement, which cannot be accomplished in its entirety without personal responsibility.

„Im Gegensatz zu den Flugzeugen können Flughäfen nicht fliegen"

gmp-Partner Hubert Nienhoff und Hans Joachim Paap, assoziierter Partner
am gmp-Standort Berlin, im Gespräch mit Architekturkritiker Jürgen Tietz

JÜRGEN TIETZ   Rückblickend auf eine lange Planungszeit, die um die Jahrtausendwende begonnen
hat …

HUBERT NIENHOFF   … 1997, im Dezember …

JT … was hat sich am Entwurf für den BER in
der Zwischenzeit verändert?

HN   Vom Testentwurf über das Planfeststellungs-
verfahren bis zur Fertigstellung hat sich an der
Grundkonstellation des Flughafens nichts Wesent-
liches verändert. Was sich verändert hat, waren die
architektonischen Ausdrucksmittel, wie zum Beispiel das Dach oder die Anbindung an eine mögliche Pier-Erweiterung.

HANS JOACHIM PAAP   Der große infrastrukturelle
Wurf, den Flughafen stadtnah zu bauen und damit
ein bestehendes System zu erweitern, ist aus heutiger Sicht völlig richtig gewesen. Dazu gehörte, eine
Bahnlinie mit S-Bahn und Airport-Express aus der
Stadt genau in die Mittelachse des Flughafens zu
legen. Es ist eigentlich der gleiche Grundgedanke
wie bei Tegel – im Zentrum des Terminals aufzutau-
chen.

JT   Also ist BER das neue Tegel?

HJP   Das ist eine Frage der Relation. Tegel bildete
ein Sechseck mit einem Durchmesser von 220 Metern. Beim BER haben wir es mit einem großen
Quadrat mit einer Kantenlänge von 750 Metern zu
tun, an das sich die Piers anschließen. Die Reisenden kommen mit Bus, Bahn oder Pkw am Willy-
Brandt-Platz an, also in der Mitte der Anlage. Daran
sind die sogenannten Prozessoren angedockt, an
denen man sein Gepäck abgibt und weiter durch
die Sicherheitskontrolle geht.

HN   Der Geist von Tegel ist weitergeführt worden –
nämlich die Idee der kurzen Wege und einer leich-
ten Orientierung für die Passagiere.

HJP   Der signifikanteste Unterschied zwischen BER
und Tegel ist, dass der neue Flughafen Teil einer
großen Infrastrukturmaßnahme ist. Heute fliegt man
anders. Dazu gehört, dass sich um den Flughafen
herum eine städtische Struktur entwickelt …

HN   … mit Hotels, Räumen für Tagungen, Parkhäu-
sern und Firmenvertretungen.

JT   Was hat sich architektonisch am Entwurf
für den BER gewandelt?

HJP   Die Veränderungen bei der architektonischen
Gestaltung hatten unter anderem mit wirtschaftli-
chen Erwägungen zu tun. Wir hatten für das Terminal zunächst ein sehr weit spannendes Dach vorgesehen, an das ein Skywalk zum Midfield-Terminal
anschließen sollte. Von geplanten 80 Metern Spann-
weite sind wir jetzt bei 42 Metern gelandet.

HN   Unser erster Entwurf für das Dach basierte auf
einem Raster von 25 Metern, um das Terminal nach
Norden und Süden modular erweitern zu können.
Die Dachkonstruktion war vorgespannt und hatte
somit eine größere Bauhöhe, jedoch mit dem Vor-
teil einer möglichst störungsfreien Bauweise im Er-
weiterungsfall. Beim zweiten Entwurf 2003/04 hatte
der Planfeststellungsbeschluss vorgegeben, dass
man nicht höher als 32 Meter über dem Vorfeld bau-
en dürfe. Das alte Dach war aber deutlich höher. Zudem gab es eine Festlegung für die Bahn.

Wir haben uns daraufhin entschieden, mit der
Schnittstelle zum Bahnhof einen unveränderbaren
Nukleus zu schaffen, der einen Orientierungspunkt
für das gesamte System bildet und über dem die
Dachscheibe schwebt, die sagt: Hier ist der Haupt-
eingang. Zur Seite war dieses System erweiterbar.
Das zweite architektonische Element neben der
schwebenden Dachscheibe waren die Kolonnaden.
Sie fassen die Vorfahrt und die Fassaden der Piers
im Norden und Süden ein.

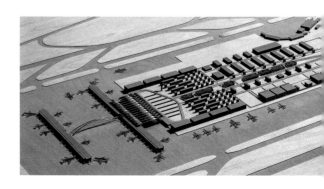

Entwurfsmodell 1998
Design model 1998

"Airports, as Opposed to Airplanes, Cannot Fly"

Hubert Nienhoff, gmp Partner, and Hans Joachim Paap, Associate Partner at gmp's Berlin office, in Conversation with Architecture Critic Jürgen Tietz

JÜRGEN TIETZ   Looking back at a long design period that started at around the turn of the millennium …
HUBERT NIENHOFF   … 1997, in December …

JT   … what has changed in the design of BER since then?
HN   From the outline design to the planning approval procedure to completion, the basic configuration of the airport has not changed significantly. What did change were the architectural means of expression, items such as the roof or the connection to a possible pier extension.
HANS JOACHIM PAAP   From today's perspective, the overarching infrastructure concept of building the airport close to the city and hence expanding an existing system was absolutely correct. This included a railway track for the metropolitan railway and Airport Express from the city running through the central axis of the airport. In a sense, it is the same basic idea as that of Tegel Airport— to arrive at the center of the terminal.

JT   So is BER the new Tegel?
HJP   That is a question of proportion. Tegel formed a hexagon with a diameter of 220 meters. BER consists of a large square with an edge length of 750 meters, plus the connecting piers. Passengers arrive by bus, railway, or car at Willy-Brandt-Platz, that is in the center of the complex. From there they proceed to the check-in facilities where you hand in your luggage, and then on through security.
HN   The spirit of Tegel has been continued—in other words, the idea of short routes and easy orientation for passengers.
HJP   The most significant difference between BER and Tegel is that the new airport is part of a large infrastructure development. These days, flying has changed. It also means that an urban structure develops around the airport …
HN   … with hotels, conference facilities, parking garages, and corporate offices.

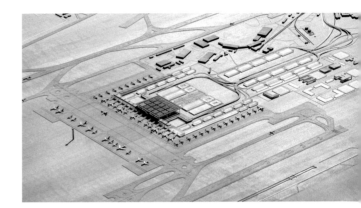

JT   Architecturally speaking, what has changed in the design for BER?
HJP   The changes in the architectural design were prompted by economic considerations, amongst others. Initially, we had intended to cover the terminal with a wide-span roof with an adjoining skywalk to the midfield terminal. From the 80-meter span we had planned, we are now left with 42 meters.
HN   Our first roof design was based on a 25-meter grid; this was chosen so that the terminal could be extended to the north and south in modular fashion. The roof construction involved a prestressed structure and therefore had a greater overall height; it had the advantage, however, of allowing relatively easy extension. Prior to the second design in 2003/04, the planning authority had stipulated that the overall building height must not exceed 32 meters measured from the apron. However, the previous roof was significantly higher. In addition, a decision was made relating to the railway.

We therefore decided to create an unchangeable nucleus at the interface with the railway station, which forms a point of orientation for the entire system and is covered by the floating roof slab that signals: here is the main entrance. This system could be extended laterally. The second architectural element in addition to the floating roof slab were the colonnades. They define the drop-off and pick-up zones, as well as the facades of the piers to the north and south.

↗ Entwurfsmodell 2004
Design model 2004

JT   Persönlich mag ich die Form der Stützen der Halle besonders gerne.

HJP   Sie entstanden, als wir mit den Ingenieuren von schlaich bergermann partner überlegten, das Dach so leicht und schwebend wie möglich zu gestalten. Das bedeutete, Pendelstützen zu bauen. Die Stützen verfügen oben und unten über ein Gelenk, das wir sichtbar halten wollten. Daraus ergab sich für die Belastung der Stützen eine Normalkraft, die das Dach trägt, und ein Knickmoment, das mit der Länge der Stütze zu tun hat. Dieses Knickmoment ist in der Mitte der Stütze am stärksten, weshalb sie sich dort aufwölbt. Kunsthistoriker würden das als Entasis bezeichnen. Insgesamt kann das Dach bei Wind bis zu 4 Zentimeter hin und her schwingen.

HN   Bei der Fassadenausbildung haben wir dann die Horizontalen betont…

HJP   …um nicht einen „Lattenzauneffekt" in der Fassade zu erzeugen. Egal, in welchem Winkel man auf die Fassade schaut, man kann von überall gut hindurchblicken.

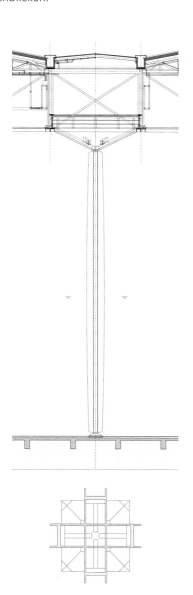

Pendelstütze in Grundriss und Schnitt
Pendulum support in plan and section

JT   Was waren die Ursachen für die Verzögerung beim Bau des Flughafens? Gab es irgendwann sogar Zweifel, dass der Flughafen überhaupt fertiggestellt würde?

HN   Nein. Diese Zweifel hatten wir nie. Man muss auch noch einmal sagen, dass eine Fertigstellung für 2012 nicht geplant war. Es sollte eine „Inbetriebnahme vor Fertigstellung" erfolgen. Die eigentliche Fertigstellung war für eineinhalb Jahre später geplant. Wir waren 2010 ja schon so gut wie fertig. Dann gab es eine ganz wesentliche Änderung, nämlich die Erweiterung des Flughafens um zwei zusätzliche Abfertigungsmodule. Das brachte die Baustelle im Terminal komplett zum Stillstand, um die Baustellenlogistik für diese Erweiterungen sicherzustellen.

HJP   2010 waren wir zeitlich guter Dinge. Der Rohbau war fertig, der Bau der Fassaden hatte begonnen. Dann kam es zu der Entscheidung, das seit 2006 geltende Verbot von Flüssigkeiten im Handgepäck zum 1.4.2013 endgültig aufzuheben. Alle Bestandsflughäfen hatten Bestandsschutz. Aber ein neues Flughafenterminal wie der BER musste die Kontrolle von mitgenommenen Flüssigkeiten gewährleisten.

Das Hauptproblem bestand dabei nicht in der Größe der Kontrollgeräte, sondern in der Fläche, die für Nachkontrollen benötigt wird und die 50 Prozent größer werden musste. Daher entschloss man sich, diese Flächen für zusätzliche Sicherheitskontrollen seitlich anzubauen, um den Verlust von Retailflächen oder Kapazitätseinbußen zu vermeiden. Damit die Passagiere aber keine weiten Wege gehen müssen, entstanden dort zudem Gepäckabgaben. Das bedeutete wiederum, dass im Zwischengeschoss zwischen Ankunft und Abflug, dort, wo die Gepäckverteilung verläuft, alles umgebaut werden musste. Diese Änderungen haben dazu geführt, dass der angedachte Termin für die Inbetriebnahme im Juni 2012 nicht gehalten werden konnte.

HN   Das alles führte zu einer Verunsicherung bei den Firmen, die durch den Stillstand teilweise wieder auf null zurückgesetzt wurden. Es mussten weltweit neue Ausschreibungen erfolgen, alles musste geplant, beantragt und genehmigt werden.

HJP   Der andere Punkt war, dass mit der Kündigung des Generalplaners alle werkvertraglichen Verpflichtungen hinfällig waren. Es galten keine Termine mehr! Alles musste neu vereinbart werden. Daraufhin wurde es ganz, ganz schwierig, und es bedurfte eines Menschen wie Engelbert Lütke Daldrup mit seiner uneitlen Ruhe und Beharrlichkeit, um es zu einem guten Ende zu bringen.

JT   Wie sehen mögliche Erweiterungsschritte aus, sobald die Covid-19-Pandemie vorbei ist und die Fluggastzahlen wieder steigen?

HN   Schon während der Planungszeit hatte sich das Bausoll nicht nur um die beiden Pavillons erweitert, sondern bereits zuvor um rund 70 Prozent – von 200.000 auf 340.000 Quadratmeter!

JT   Personally, I really like the shape of the columns of the hall.

HJP   This was the outcome of our deliberations with the engineers from schlaich bergermann partner, when attempting to design the roof as lightweight and floating as possible. This resulted in our choice of hinged columns. These columns have a hinged joint at the top and bottom, something that we wanted to be visible. The forces acting on the columns consist of the normal force from supporting the roof and a buckling moment related to the length of the column. This buckling moment is strongest at the center of the column, which is why they have this slightly convex shape. Art historians would refer to this as entasis. In high winds, the roof can move to and fro by up to 4 centimeters.

HN   In the facade design we emphasized the horizontal…

HJP   …in order to avoid creating a palisade effect in the facade. You have a clear view through the facade, regardless of the angle from which you look at it.

JT   What was the cause for the delay in the construction of the airport? Did any doubts arise at any stage as to whether the airport would ever be completed?

HN   No. We never had these doubts. It is also important to remember that completion had not been scheduled for 2012. What had been planned was that the airport would start operations before completion. The actual completion had been planned for eighteen months later. In 2010, we were in fact very close to completion. Then a very significant change was stipulated, namely the extension of the airport by two additional check-in modules. That meant that all construction activities in the terminal had to stop in order to allow for the construction site logistics of the extensions.

HJP   In 2010, we were in good spirits in terms of the schedule. The shell construction was complete, construction of the facades had been started. Then the decision was taken to finally allow passengers, as of April 1, 2013, to take liquids onboard—something that had been prohibited since 2006. All existing airports were unaffected. But any new airport terminal, such as BER, had to made provision for screening liquids.

  The main problem was not the size of the control equipment, but the space required in the post-control area, which had to be increased by 50 percent. In this context it was decided to add the space for additional security controls laterally in order to avoid losing retail area or reducing capacity. At the same time, baggage check-in points were created here in order to save passengers from having to walk long distances. In turn, this meant that everything had to be changed in the mezzanine floor between arrivals and departures, where baggage distribution takes place. All these changes led to the planned opening date in June 2012 being missed.

HN   All this resulted in uncertainty amongst the contractors, some of whose contracts had to be voided due to the halt in construction. A new worldwide tendering procedure had to be started, and everything had to be planned, applied for, and approved.

HJP   The other point was that, following the termination of the general contractor contract, all obligations under existing work contracts became null and void. The existing deadlines no longer applied! Everything had to be renegotiated. After that everything became very, very difficult and it needed a person such as Engelbert Lütke Daldrup, with his immense calmness and perseverance, to bring this to a good conclusion.

JT   What are possible expansion steps once the Covid 19 pandemic is over and passenger numbers are increasing again?

HN   Even during the design phase, in addition to the two pavilions, the stipulated space requirement was increased by about 70 percent—from 200,000 to 340,000 square meters!

HJP   We started with a system design totaling an area of 220,000 square meters and were then tasked with reducing the budget and area by 10 percent. By 2012, it had increased to 340,000 square meters, part of which had been added during the construction process. It is crazy that this worked at all!

HN   Coming back to the options for extending the airport: BER airport has sufficient reserves for a long time. If peak capacity is ever reached, it is possible to add passenger piers with separate check-in facilities. This would make it possible to increase the number of passengers from currently 32 million to about 40 to 45 million.

HJP   However, at this capacity and given the aircraft mix at BER—with few wide-bodied aircraft as compared to Frankfurt, Munich, or Heathrow—a third runway is gradually becoming necessary. This is the real contradiction. Avoiding the hub function means that more aircraft are needed to handle the number of passengers. In the future, this is something politicians will have to address.

↑ Dach der Check-in-Halle im Bau
  Roof of the check-in hall under construction

HJP   Wir sind mit einem Systementwurf von 220.000 Quadratmetern Fläche gestartet und hatten die Aufgabe, davon 10 Prozent Budget und Fläche einzusparen. 2012 standen dann die 340.000 Quadratmeter, die teilweise während des Bauprozesses hinzugekommen waren. Verrückt, dass das überhaupt funktioniert hat!

HN   Noch einmal zurück zur Frage der Erweiterungsmöglichkeiten: Der Flughafen BER besitzt noch für lange Zeit ausreichend Reserven. Wenn dort jemals die Spitzen erreicht werden, können zusätzliche Abfertigungspiers mit separaten Abfertigungs-Check-ins angedockt werden. Das ermöglicht eine nochmalige Steigerung von derzeit 32 auf 40 bis 45 Millionen Passagiere.

HJP   Bei dieser Kapazität und dem Berliner Flugzeugmix, mit wenigen Großraumflugzeugen im Vergleich zu Frankfurt, München oder Heathrow, braucht es allerdings langsam eine dritte Start- und Landebahn. Das ist der eigentliche Widerspruch. Die Vermeidung der Hubfunktion führt zu mehr Flugbewegungen im Originärverkehr. Damit wird sich die Politik in Zukunft auseinandersetzen müssen.

JT   Gehören Flughäfen zu den komplexesten Bauaufgaben, die es im Moment gibt? Oder sind sie eigentlich ganz einfach, wenn man sie beherrscht?

HJP   Das Problem ist, dass ein Flughafen kein einzelnes Gebäude ist, sondern eher einen Prozess darstellt. Dazu gehören Einzelaspekte wie die infrastrukturelle Anbindung: Wie kommen die Leute zum Flughafen? Soll es einen richtig großen Bahnhof geben oder nur einen S-Bahnhof? Hinzu kommen die Auf- und Rückgabe des Reisegepäcks und die Sicherheitskontrollen für Gepäck und Menschen.

Ein weiterer wichtiger wirtschaftlicher Aspekt ist die „goldene Stunde" an Flughäfen. Man bedient sich der schnellsten Art der Fortbewegung, indem man durch die Luft fliegt und dadurch Zeit sparen will. Aber der Mensch ist unsicher und ängstlich und baut sich bestimmte Puffer ein. Wenn aber alles gut läuft, braucht er seine Puffer nicht auf und sagt sich, „Mensch, jetzt habe ich eine halbe Stunde Zeit." Wenn man in diesem Moment die richtigen Kaufanreize setzt, geben die Leute viel Geld aus, weil sie entspannt sind. Das nennt der Flughafenbetreiber die goldene Stunde – oder auch nur die goldene halbe Stunde. Das alles zusammenzubringen, also den Wandel in der Verkehrsmodalität, die Trennung und Zuführung von Gepäck, die Orientierung im System, damit ich schnell meinen Flug finde, und diese Überlagerung mit Food/Beverage und Retail macht die Bauaufgabe Flughafen komplex.

HN   Viele Flughäfen in Deutschland, aber auch weltweit bilden ja aufgrund ihrer Entstehungsgeschichte ein Patchwork, sodass die Menschen leicht die Orientierung verlieren. Der Flughafen Heathrow war dafür über viele Jahre bekannt. Wenn man das alles bedenkt und aus diesen Fehlern lernt und die Psychologie im Verhalten der Nutzerinnen und Nutzer beachtet, dann ist es schon sehr komplex.

JT   Sind Flughäfen wie der BER „Nicht-Orte", wie sie Marc Augé einmal genannt hat?

HN   Es war unsere Absicht, dass mit dem BER ein Ort entsteht, der wiedererkennbar ist, der sich mit der Umgebung und allen Abläufen an dieser Stelle vernetzt und den Menschen eine Orientierung gibt. Wir wollten ein Gebäude entwerfen, das so nur hier stehen kann.

HJP   Eine der zentralen Aufgaben im Wettbewerb 2004 war es, eine Ortsidentität zu schaffen. Uns war es wichtig, dass der Mensch hier Erfahrungen macht, die er mit Berlin verbindet. Dazu gehören auch die Materialien, das Nussbaumholz oder der Jura-Kalkstein.

Darüber hinaus war es uns wichtig, dass man immer aus dem Flughafen in die Umgebung schauen kann. Wenn ich in dem Pier entlanggehe, sehe ich auf der einen Seite Flugzeuge und weiß, dort steige ich ein. Schaue ich auf der anderen Seite hinaus, sehe ich Autos. Dort geht es also zur Landseite.

HN   Am Anfang, als wir noch keinen Strich für den Entwurf gemacht hatten, haben wir die formale Entscheidung getroffen, dem Flughafen keine Assoziationen mit auf den Weg zu geben, die in irgendeiner Weise mit dem Fliegen spielen. Im Gegensatz zu den Flugzeugen auf dem Rollfeld können Flughäfen schließlich nicht fliegen. Deswegen sollte es ein geerdeter Ort werden. Ein Ort, an dem man gut ankommt und sich wohlfühlt.

JT   Der vielleicht geerdetste Ort des Flughafens ist der Raum der Stille. Inwieweit ist er Teil der Identität des Flughafens?

HJP   Normalerweise sind Räume der Stille eher versteckt. Beim BER befindet er sich in der absoluten Öffentlichkeit, gut auffindbar in der Zentralachse des Gesamtsystems, an der Schnittstelle zwischen Luft- und Landseite. Unsere Idee war, dass der Raum ein integratives Moment besitzen sollte und für alle Weltreligionen da ist. Daher haben wir keinen einzelnen Raum entworfen, sondern eine Raumfolge. Was diese Räume vereint, ist der Himmel, den man erahnt, wenn man durch ein Oculus nach oben schaut. Alle schauen in den gleichen Himmel und haben im Prinzip das gleiche Ansinnen.

Weil die alten Kirchen in Berlin und Brandenburg aus Ziegel bestehen, haben wir ebenfalls Ziegel verwendet. Alles wurde in Form und Material reduziert und für die Noblesse lediglich ein bisschen Bronze hinzugefügt. Wir waren sehr glücklich, dass der Vertrag für den Raum der Stille nie gekündigt wurde. Ich durfte 2020 die Fertigstellungsanzeige an das Amt schicken, Landkreis Dahme-Spreewald in Königs Wusterhausen. So hat sich alles gefügt. Mit dem lieben Gott treibt man keinen Schabernack.

JT   Are airports amongst the most complex de-sign tasks? Or are they really quite simple once you are familiar with them?

HJP   The problem is that an airport is not a single building but rather represents a process. This in-volves a number of separate aspects, such as the landside transport infrastructure: how do people get to the airport? Should there be a really large railway station or just a metropolitan line station? Then there are the baggage check-in and baggage claim areas and the security controls for luggage and people.

Another important economic aspect is the "golden hour" at airports. People choose the fastest mode of transport, intending to save time by flying through the air. At the same time, people are in-secure and fearful and like to plan certain time buf-fers. However, when everything goes well, they don't need the extra time and say "Gosh, I have half an hour to myself."

When you provide the right purchase incen-tives at this moment, people spend a lot of money because they are relaxed. That's what airport opera-tors call the golden hour—or even the golden half hour. Bringing all these aspects together, namely the change in transport mode, the drop-off and col-lection of luggage, the orientation in the system to ensure that people find their flight quickly, and the additional superimposition with food/beverage and retail outlets, makes the design of an airport a com-plex task.

HN   Owing to their historical development, many airports in Germany—and worldwide—look like patchworks, which means that people easily lose orientation. Heathrow Airport was well known for this for many years. When you take all this into con-sideration and learn from these mistakes, and also take into account the psychology of the user behavior, you end up with a very complex task.

JT   Are airports such as BER "non-places," as Marc Augé called them once?

HN   Our intention with BER was to create a place that is recognizable, that interacts with its environ-ment and all related processes, and that helps peo-ple with their orientation. We wanted to design a building that can only be created here in this way.

HJP   One of the key tasks in the 2004 competition was to create a local identity. For us it was important that people have an experience here that they associate with Berlin. The materials, such as walnut wood and Jura limestone, are part of that.

In addition, we felt it was important that you could always look out from the airport to view the surroundings. When I walk along the pier, I see air-craft on one side and know that this is where I have to board. When I look out on the other side, I see cars. So that is where you get to the landside.

HN   At the beginning, before we had drawn a sin-gle line, we made the formal decision not to charge the airport with any associations connected with flying. After all, Airports, as opposed to airplanes on the tarmac, cannot fly. Therefore, we wanted it to be a grounded place. A place at which you arrive well and where you feel well.

JT   Perhaps the most grounded room in the air-port is the Room of Silence. To what extent is it part of the airport's identity?

HJP   Normally, rooms of silence tend to be hidden away. At BER it is in a very public location; it is easy to find along the central axis of the overall system, at the interface between the airside and landside. We felt that the room should have an integrating el-ement and be available to all world religions. For this reason, we did not design a single room but a sequence of rooms. What unifies these rooms is the sky that you may just make out when you look up through an oculus. All visitors look at the same sky and, generally speaking, share the same purpose.

We used brick in the design because all the old churches in Berlin and Brandenburg are built of brick. Everything was reduced in terms of shape and material, and the only classy addition was a little bit of bronze. We were very happy about the fact that our contract for the design of the Room of Silence was never terminated. In 2020, I had the privilege of sending the completion notice to the office of the Dahme-Spreewald Rural District in Königs Wuster-hausen. So everything fell into place. You don't play games with God.

↖   Visualisierung Raum der Stille
     Rendering of the Room of Silence

„Die Politik als Bauherr hat versagt"

Der lange Leidensweg des Hauptstadtflughafens BER

Falk Jaeger

Großprojekte wie der Flughafen BER oder Stuttgart 21 sind in wachsendem Maß Gegenstand kontroverser öffentlicher Diskurse. Die Bedingungen, auf die solch komplexe Bauvorhaben bei Planung und Realisierung treffen, werden immer schwieriger, zuweilen unüberwindbar, so gesehen beim Transrapid zum Münchner Flughafen. Die Folgen sind haarsträubende Bauverzögerungen wie etwa bei der Rheintalstrecke der Bahnlinie Rotterdam – St. Gotthard – Genua und/oder erhebliche Kostensteigerungen wie bei der Elbphilharmonie.

Der Fahrplan des Scheiterns ist immer der gleiche: Ein politischer Baubeschluss wird herbeigeführt, ohne dass die Beschlussgrundlagen vorliegen, das genaue Programm, die Baubedingungen und eine realistische Kostenschätzung. Dann entdeckt der öffentliche Bauherr seine Lust am Bauen, definiert das Programm und greift später beherzt in die laufenden Planungen und Baumaßnahmen ein. Dann stellt sich heraus, dass sich alles „unvorhersehbar" verteuert. Dann hat man schon angefangen und glaubte, den Point of no Return überschritten zu haben. Zu Deutsch: Augen zu und durch.

Hinzu kommen neue gesellschaftliche Einflüsse. Unmittelbar und mittelbar Betroffene, Umweltverbände und viele andere haben Einspruchsrechte, die so manches Projekt ins Wanken bringen.

Bei alledem hat die öffentliche Meinung, hat die Medienberichterstattung eine Schlüsselrolle inne. Nur: Die Großprojekte haben eine Komplexität erreicht, die kein Außenstehender, auch kein Journalist zu durchschauen vermag. Vor allem Verantwortlichkeiten lassen sich im Dickicht der Zuständigkeitskaskaden, der Planungs-, Genehmigungs- und Kontrollfunktionen kaum mehr ausmachen.

So kommt es, dass die Presse von den Protagonisten leicht hinters Licht geführt werden kann. Der BER war ein Paradebeispiel dafür, wie es gelingt, durch geschickte Öffentlichkeitsarbeit von den eigentlichen Problemen abzulenken und der Presse nebensächliche Skandälchen durchzustechen, an denen sie sich abarbeiten kann. Das heißt nicht viel weniger, als dass die Presse als „vierte Gewalt" und gesellschaftliches Kontrollorgan zumindest in den ersten Jahren ebenso versagte wie die Politik bei ihren ureigensten Kontrollfunktionen.

Ein typischer Effekt ist die reflexhafte Schuldzuweisung bei Bauvorhaben. Für Journalisten, die im Bauwesen nicht bewandert sind und von Begriffen wie Planung, Projektleitung, Generalunternehmer, Generalübernehmer, Bauleitung, Projektsteuerung, Bauaufsicht, Baugenehmigung, Tragwerksplanung, TGA und so weiter keine präzise Vorstellung haben, ist bei einer Baustelle, bei der es im Argen liegt, immer der Architekt der Schuldige. In dieser Überzeugung fühlte sich die Presse speziell beim BER bestätigt, als die Architekten auch vom Bauherrn als die Schuldigen präsentiert und aus dem Projekt entlassen wurden. Erst durch Fachpresseartikel und Einrede vonseiten der nichtinvolvierten Fachwelt erkannte die Publikumspresse etwa ab Mitte 2012 langsam, wer eigentlich Verantwortung trug und welche gravierenden Auswirkungen die ungerechtfertigte Entlassung haben würde. Die Journalisten der Leitmedien haben Jahre gebraucht, um sich in das Projekt einzuarbeiten und einigermaßen unabhängig (und zutreffend) über die Vorgänge am BER berichten und sie beurteilen zu können.

Das Projekt „Großflughafen Berlin" stand von Anbeginn unter keinem guten Stern. Das betrifft die Standortwahl, die aus politischen Gründen auf das zu kleine (nur zwei Landebahnen) und aus Gründen des Fluglärmschutzes ungünstige Areal am Flughafen Schönefeld fiel. Das betrifft die diversen Privatisierungsverfahren, mit deren Hilfe man Planer und Unternehmer aussuchen wollte. Und das betrifft die Unklarheiten über die Bemessungsgrößen und Dimensionierung des Terminals, die sich mehrfach, sogar noch während der Bauphase, änderten und kostspielige Umplanungen und Umbauten nach sich zogen.

Der Wettbewerb um den Bauauftrag und die Konstituierung eines Finanzierungs- und Betreibermodells hätten schlechter kaum laufen können. Der umstrittenen Auswahl von Hochtief mit dem Entwurf von gmp folgte aus Angst vor langwierigen Rechtsstreitigkeiten die zwangsweise Kooperation mit dem Konkurrenten IVG Immobilien AG, wonach der nunmehr einzige Anbieter postwendend sein Angebot in die Höhe trieb. Die Privatisierung des Projekts wurde deshalb nicht weiterverfolgt. Die Bauherren Land Berlin, Land Brandenburg und Minderheitenanteilseigner Bund beschlossen, mit ihrer Flughafengesellschaft selbst zu bauen. Das erwies sich aus heutiger Sicht aus zwei Gründen als epochaler Fehler. Das ursprüngliche Komplettangebot des Generalübernehmers ist durch die tatsächlichen Kosten am Ende um ein Mehrfaches übertroffen worden. Außerdem war der Bauherr nie in der Lage, den für ein solches Megaprojekt notwendigen Sachverstand auf Planungs-, Organisations- und Finanzierungsebene zu rekrutieren.

"The Failure of Politicians as Clients"

The Long Ordeal of BER, the Capital's Airport

Mega-projects such as BER Airport or Stuttgart 21 have increasingly become the subject of public controversy. The conditions pertaining to such complex building projects in terms of design and construction are becoming more and more difficult; at times the problems are insurmountable, as could be seen with the Transrapid link to Munich Airport. The consequences are either huge delays in construction, such as those seen at the Rhine Valley route of the Rotterdam-St. Gotthard-Genoa railway line, and/or enormous cost increases such as those of the Elbphilharmonie concert hall in Hamburg.

The pattern of failure is always the same: a political decision is made in favor of the project without any precise details, such as the exact brief, planning conditions, and a realistic cost estimate. Then the public clients discover their penchant for building, they define the brief and, at a later date, massively interfere with the ongoing design and construction process. Thereafter, it turns out that everything has become "unpredictably" more expensive. At this point, construction work has already begun, and it is believed that a point of no return has passed. In short: Press on regardless!

Then there are new influencing factors raised by the people at large. Directly and indirectly affected stakeholders, environmental associations, and many others have the right to object, which can derail many a project.

On top of all that, public opinion, as represented by media reporting, plays a key role. However, these mega-projects have reached such a degree of complexity that no outsider, and no journalist, can see the entire picture. In particular, the thicket of cascading responsibilities, of planning, approval, and control functions, makes it almost impossible to discern who is responsible for what.

As a result, the press is easily misled by the protagonists. BER is a prime example of how to distract from the real problems through clever public relations work, of how to feed the press minor scandals on which they can go to work. This really means that—at least in the initial years—the press as a "fourth force" and social control mechanism failed to the same degree as the political institutions did in their mandatory control function.

Typically, the reflex reaction is to apportion blame in building projects. Journalists who are not familiar with the building industry and who have no exact idea of the meaning of terms such as planning, design, project management, general contractor, design & build contractor, site supervision, project control, building approval, structural design, MEP and so on, always think that, if a construction project encounters problems, the architect is to blame. In this conviction the press felt particularly vindicated in the case of BER, because the clients also presented the architects as being those to blame and dismissed them from the project. It was not until articles appeared in professional journals and uninvolved professionals raised objections that the public press, from around 2012, slowly understood who really was responsible and what grave effects the unjustified dismissal would have. It took journalists of the leading media years to work their way into the project until they were able to report at least somewhat independently (and accurately) on events at BER—and capable of forming an opinion about them.

From the very beginning, the "Berlin mega-airport" project encountered serious hurdles. A particular case in point, is the choice of the location which, for political reasons, was made in favor of the area of Schönefeld Airport, which is too small (only two runways) and unfavorable for reasons of noise pollution. Another case in point is the various privatization procedures via which professional consultants and contractors were to be appointed. Yet another case in point is the lack of clarity regarding the size of the terminal, which was revised several times even during the construction phase and resulted in very costly redesigns and reconstruction.

The competitive tendering for the building contract and the establishment of a funding and operating model could hardly have been any more inefficient. For fear of extensive litigation, the contentious selection of Hochtief with the gmp design (as sole contractor) was dropped in favor of a mandatory cooperation with their competitor, IVG Immobilien AG, which predictably resulted in this now sole bidder driving up the bid price. For this reason, privatization of the project was abandoned. The clients, consisting of the State of Berlin, the State of Brandenburg, and the Federal Government as minority shareholder decided to undertake the project themselves via their "Flughafengesellschaft" (Airport Corporation). From today's perspective, this has turned out to be a monstrous mistake for two reasons. In the end, the actual cost was a multiple of the original inclusive bid price for the overall project by the design & build contractor. Furthermore, the

Offenkundig sind große, international agierende Bauträger mit eingespielten Führungsstrukturen und ihrem Fachverstand auf allen Managementebenen als Bauherr einer Flughafengesellschaft um Längen voraus, deren Führungsstruktur vom Jagdglück der Headhunter abhängt.

Bei Planung und Bau des BER war ein planvolles, routiniertes, effektives Zusammenarbeiten all die Jahre nicht möglich, weil man sich permanent im Krisenmodus befand. Unter solchen Bedingungen neigen Verantwortliche zu defensivem Handeln, um sich abzusichern, was wiederum offene Kommunikation erschwert. Entscheidungen über Planungen, Auftragsvergaben und Kontrollmechanismen der Flughafengesellschaft und die Arbeit der anderen Beteiligten wurden mit den Architekten nicht kommuniziert. Ein Bauvorhaben dieser Größenordnung, bei dem den Akteuren jeweils nur Teilwissen zugestanden wird, kann nicht reibungslos ablaufen. Dieser Zustand hat sich erst ab 2017 mit dem offeneren Führungsstil des neuen Vorsitzenden der Geschäftsführung Engelbert Lütke Daldrup geändert, eine Voraussetzung für die letztendlich geglückte Fertigstellung des Projekts.

Eine der größten Herausforderungen für die Architekten bestand darin, dass die Prognosen über den zukünftigen Umfang des Flugverkehrs und die daraus resultierende Bemessung der Kapazität während des ganzen Planungsprozesses umstritten waren. Vor München II hatte sich die Lufthansa den BER als Drehkreuz gewünscht, mit vielen Fernverbindungen, wie sie der Regierende Bürgermeister Klaus Wowereit noch lange anstrebte (A380). Als dann Schönefeld als Standort feststand, sah die Politik den BER neben den „Großflughäfen" Frankfurt und München nur noch als „Regionalflughafen". Aufwendige Änderungsanträge blieben nicht aus.

Als die Kosten für die 220.000 Quadratmeter des Terminals erstmals genauer kalkuliert waren und weit über dem Budget lagen, erging an die Planer der Auftrag, die Fläche um 20.000 Quadratmeter zu reduzieren. Die Terminalhalle wurde gegenüber dem Erstentwurf um zwei der sieben Raummodule verkleinert. Übrigens mussten 2009, als im weiteren Fortgang der Flächenbedarf wieder stieg, zwei „Pavillons" nördlich und südlich des Terminals ergänzt werden – just anstelle der zwei zuvor eingesparten Module. Verschärfte Sicherheitsrichtlinien der EU wurden als Grund angegeben, die mehr Platz für Personenkontrollen erforderten.

Eine besondere Herausforderung war auch die Vorgabe des Bauherrn, die EU-Verordnung im Hinblick auf die Trennung der Verkehrswege der Passagiere mit Non-Schengen- und Schengen-Status bei gleichbleibender Kubatur zu realisieren. Eine Zwischenebene musste dafür in das Terminal eingefügt werden, was eine Kette von erheblichen Bauänderungen nach sich zog wie eine verringerte Geschosshöhe im Erdgeschoss, Anpassung der haustechnischen Anlagen und vieles mehr. Mehr Fläche und Funktionen bei gleichem Bauvolumen bedeuten beengtere Verhältnisse in den Kabel- und Lüftungskanälen. Das sollte sich rächen.

Ursprünglich war der Non-Schengen-Abflugbereich im Zentrum des Terminals vorgesehen, zugänglich von beiden Airline-Allianzen, One World vom Südbereich des Hauptpiers, Star Alliance vom Nordbereich. Im Zentrum des Terminals waren Gate-Positionen für das Großraumflugzeug A380 geplant, wahlweise bedient vom Lufthansa- oder vom Air-Berlin-Bereich. Als die Lufthansa beteuerte, nicht mit dem A380 nach Berlin zu fliegen, verschwanden die A380-Positionen aus den Plänen. Später sollte auf ausdrücklichen Wunsch des Regierenden Bürgermeisters doch ein A380-Gate eingeplant werden – für die Air Berlin. Dazu musste die Brücke in den Abfertigungsbereich von Air Berlin an das Südende des Hauptpiers verschoben werden; sie liegt also außerhalb des Non-Schengen-Bereichs. „Ebenenshift" nannten die Architekten die notwendigen Umplanungen. Einreisekontrollen, Transferstationen und entsprechende Passagierführungen samt zusätzlichen Rettungswegen auf allen Geschossen mussten umgeplant werden, ohne die Kubatur zu verändern. Die Air Berlin hatte freilich noch kein Flugzeug dieses Typs bestellt und verabschiedete sich später ohnehin aus dem Markt. Da die Airlines den A380 inzwischen ausmustern, wird das doppelgeschossige Gate wohl niemals gebraucht werden.

Mitte 2006 brachte der neue Geschäftsbereich Non-Aviation seine Anforderungen in das Projekt ein. Zentraler Angelpunkt des neuen Retailkonzepts war der vergrößerte „Walk Through Shop", durch den alle Passagiere direkt nach der Sicherheitskontrolle geführt werden. Aus diesem Grunde musste die komplette Abflugebene des Terminals umgeplant werden. Neben der Zentralisierung der Sicherheitskontrollen und des Zugangs zur Luftseite wurden auch die luftseitigen Retailflächen zulasten der Check-in-Halle erweitert. Dies führte zu mehr profitablen Flächen auf der Luftseite, jedoch auch zur Reduktion von Check-in-Schaltern und Abfertigungskapazität sowie zu höheren Brandlasten. Ebenfalls als der Rohbau schon im Gang war, entschied der Aufsichtsrat, die zuvor aus Kostengründen gestrichenen Laufbänder nachzurüsten, wiederum mit erheblichen Folgen für Rohbau und technische Gebäudeausrüstung.

Wenngleich die Baukosten zügig anstiegen und der Eröffnungstermin immer weiter in die Zukunft rückte, lagen die 487 Planänderungen nach Wünschen des Bauherrn bis 2010 noch im Bereich des Beherrschbaren. Das änderte sich grundlegend, als der Termin für die Inbetriebnahme im Juni 2012 näher rückte und zu platzen drohte. Die Flughafengesellschaft ordnete „Baubeschleunigungsmaßnahmen" an und verließ den Weg der koordinierenden Projektleitung und des Controllings. Freihändige Beauftragungen von Firmen ohne präzise vorgegebene Pläne und ohne deren operative Einbindung in den Bauprozess führten zu einem unkontrollierbaren Zustand von Projekt, Zuständigkeiten und Baustelle.

Als der in den vergangenen Jahren bereits mehrfach verschobene, aber diesmal sehr konkret organisierte Termin 3. Juni 2012 abgesagt werden musste, sahen sich die Verantwortlichen veranlasst, einen Schuldigen zu präsentieren. Der Aufsichtsratsvorsitzende, Berlins Regierender Bürgermeister Klaus Wowereit, verkündete

clients were never able to recruit the personnel required for such a huge project in terms of design, organization, and funding expertise.

It is quite obvious that, in the role as building client, large international contractors with seasoned management structures and professional expertise at all management levels are miles ahead of an airport corporation, the management structure of which largely depends on the headhunters' luck.

During the design and construction of BER, planned, well-versed, and effective cooperation was not possible throughout the years because the project was permanently in crisis mode. In such circumstances, those responsible tend to act defensively in order to cover their backs, which in turn is detrimental to open communication. The decisions of the Flughafengesellschaft about planned steps, the assignment of contracts, control mechanisms, and the work of the other participants were not communicated to the architects. A building project of this size, in which key players are only given partial information, can never run smoothly. This situation did not change until, in 2017, the new Chairman of the Management Board, Engelbert Lütke Daldrup, established a new open management style, a prerequisite for the ultimately successful completion of the project.

One of the biggest challenges for the architects was the fact that the projection of the future volume of air traffic and the resulting airport capacity continued to be argued about throughout the design process. Prior to Munich II, Lufthansa had hoped to establish BER as its hub with many long-haul destinations, and this was also pursued for a long time by Berlin's Governing Mayor, Klaus Wowereit (A380). When, finally, the decision was made in favor of Schönefeld, politicians regarded BER merely as a "regional airport" rather than a "major airport" like Frankfurt and Munich. Applications for costly modifications did not fail to materialize.

When the costs for the 220,000 square meters of the terminal were precisely calculated for the first time and they far exceeded the budget, the architects were tasked with reducing the area by 20,000 square meters. Compared to the initial design, the terminal hall was reduced by two of the seven spatial modules. Then, in 2009, when the need for more floor area was gradually recognized, two "pavilions" had to be added to the north and south of the terminal—thus replacing the two modules that had previously been removed. The reason given was stricter EU security guidelines that required more space for passenger control.

Another particular challenge was the clients' request to satisfy the EU regulation regarding the separation of non-Schengen and Schengen passenger routes without increasing the volume of the terminal space. This meant that a mezzanine level had to be inserted in the terminal, which resulted in a series of substantial modifications, changed services installations, reduced height of the first floor, and much else. When more functions have to be accommodated in the same building volume, there is less space available for the necessary cable and ventilation ducts. That caused further problems.

Originally, the non-Schengen departure area had been placed at the center of the terminal with access from both airline alliances: One World from south of the main pier and Star Alliance from the north. Gate positions for the wide-bodied A380 aircraft had been planned at the center of the terminal, to be serviced from the Lufthansa or Air Berlin zones. When Lufthansa confirmed that it would not use the A380 to fly to Berlin, the A380 positions disappeared from the plans. Later, upon express request from the Governing Mayor, an A380 gate was to be included in the design—for Air Berlin. To make this possible, the jetbridge had to be moved to the Air Berlin check-in area at the south end of the main pier, i.e., outside the non-Schengen area. The architects called the necessary redesigns "Ebenenshift" [level shift]. Entry controls, transfer stations, and the respective passenger routes, including all additional escape routes, had to be redesigned on all floors without changing the overall building volume. There was, of course, the small matter that Air Berlin had not actually ordered an aircraft of this type and, in any case, later quit the market. In view of the fact that the airlines have now decided to abandon the A380, the double-story gate will probably never be used.

By the middle of 2006, the new non-aviation business division announced its own requirements. The key point of the new retail concept was the larger "walk-through shop," which all passengers had to pass through directly after security control. For this reason, the entire departure level of the terminal had to be redesigned. In addition to centralizing the security checks and the access to the air side, the retail areas on the airside were also extended, taking space from the check-in hall. This led to more profitable areas on the airside but also to a reduction in the number of check-in desks and in handling capacity, as well as an increase in potential fire loads. Furthermore, when shell construction was already underway, the Supervisory Board decided to install the moving walkways after all, even though they had previously been scrapped for cost reasons. This led to major changes to the shell construction and building services.

Even though the construction costs were rising rapidly and the opening date moved further and further into the future, the 487 changes to the plans requested by the clients up until 2010 were still within manageable limits. That changed drastically when the opening date of June 2012 moved closer and was likely to fall through. Flughafengesellschaft ordered "speeding-up measures," abandoning coordinated project management and controlling. Companies were commissioned without precise plans and without obligation to cooperate in the general building process, which led to an uncontrollable situation with respect to the project, responsibilities, and construction site.

When the opening date of June 3, 2012—which in previous years had been postponed several times but this time was organized in great detail—had to be cancelled, those in charge felt compelled to present a culprit. On

am 23. Mai 2012 im Habitus des Machers, der nun das Heft in die Hand nimmt, die Entlassung des Planerteams.

Die Tragweite dieser Entscheidung war Fachleuten, aber auch anderen Beobachtern sofort klar. Aus dem GAU wurde ein Super-GAU. Der Rauswurf des gesamten Projekt- und Sachstandwissens kostete in der Folge mehrere Jahre Zeit und hunderte Millionen Euro zusätzlich. Zwar erweckte das Gebäude den Anschein, als ob es bis auf ein paar Retuschen fertig wäre und die Architekten ihre Entwurfsarbeit eigentlich getan hätten und man nur noch einige Sicherheits- und Brandschutzanlagen zum Laufen bringen müsse. Viele rechneten also mit einer weiteren Verzögerung von einigen Monaten oder höchstens einem Jahr. Die technischen Probleme erwiesen sich jedoch als gravierend. Und nun mussten projektfremde Teams ohne werkvertragliche Verpflichtung ins Boot geholt werden, die dann nach Aufwand entlohnt wurden. Diese Teams arbeiteten sich einerseits monatelang in das komplexe Bauvorhaben ein und versuchten andererseits, durch eine Bestandsaufnahme den undokumentierten Wildwuchs zu durchleuchten. Die Entrauchungsanlage hatte sich durch die Umbauten bis zur Unbeherrschbarkeit verkompliziert. Kabelkanäle waren falsch besetzt und überbelegt, Brandabschnittsgrenzen waren unbedacht durchbrochen, unzertifizierte Bauteile eingebaut worden. Die Software der Sicherheitsanlagen war überfordert. Von der Erlangung der Betriebsgenehmigung war man weit entfernt. Viele Anlagen wurden ausgebaut und neu installiert, manche sogar zweimal.

Im Nachhinein ist klar, dass 2012 eine Radikallösung rascher und billiger zum Ziel geführt hätte: nicht Umplanung und Umbau, sondern Herausreißen, Neuplanung und Neubau der gesamten Installationen des Terminals. Stattdessen versuchten mehrere Nachfolger des gescheiterten Geschäftsführers und mehrere Technikvorstände sowie zahlreiche Planungsfirmen, externe Berater und Controller, das Projekt in den Griff zu bekommen. Sie scheiterten alle daran, dass es keine verlässlichen Pläne mehr gab und somit keine bindenden Verträge mit den Firmen mit festen Termin- und Preisvereinbarungen möglich waren. Die Firmen waren nur bereit, risikolos auf Zuruf und auf Stundenbasis zu arbeiten - mit den erwartbaren Konsequenzen für Kosten und Termine.

Schließlich gelang es dem 2017 neu berufenen Vorsitzenden der Geschäftsführung, Engelbert Lütke Daldrup, das Projekt wieder auf eine solide Grundlage zu stellen. Er schaffte es, alle bis dahin mehr gegen- als miteinander agierenden Protagonisten auf die gemeinsame Sache einzuschwören und Ordnung in die Planungen und vor allem in das Vertragswesen zu bringen.

Kein neuer Eröffnungstermin wurde benannt. Erst mussten genügend Sicherheiten geschaffen werden, um dann verkünden zu können: Am 31. Oktober 2020 wird der erste Flieger landen, planmäßig, aber mit achtjähriger Verspätung.

Dass Lütke Daldrup für größere Feierlichkeiten keinen Anlass sah und den neuen Airport in aller Stille seiner Bestimmung übergab, war nach der endlosen Kette von Fehlern, Versäumnissen und Skandalen und dem finanziellen Desaster verständlich. Dass die Eröffnung in die Zeit der Coronapandemie fiel und deshalb der Flugverkehr auf niedrigstem Niveau sehr langsam anlief, hatte immerhin sein Gutes, konnten sich doch alle betrieblichen Systeme stressfrei einspielen.

Nachdem der Pulverdampf verzogen ist, kann der neue Flughafen nun endlich seine funktionalen Vorzüge im Betrieb unter Beweis stellen. Und vielleicht kann auch seine Architektur vorurteilsfrei betrachtet werden. Wenn das Bauvorhaben auch architektonisch zu einem guten Ende gebracht werden konnte, so ist die langfristige Finanzierung der Flughafengesellschaft wegen des Schuldenbergs noch nicht in trockenen Tüchern.

Die Frage, was die Gesellschaft für künftige Großvorhaben daraus lernen kann, was man hätte besser und richtig machen können, ist angesichts des multiplen Organversagens nicht leicht zu beantworten. Vielleicht so viel: Das Projekt muss seriös durchgeplant und realistisch kalkulierbar sein, bevor überhaupt ein politischer Baubeschluss mit Budgetierung erfolgt. Die Bauherrschaft muss in professionelle Hände übergeben werden, zum Beispiel einem potenten Konsortium mit internationaler Expertise, das Kosten und Termine zu garantieren hat. Die Politik muss sich aus dem weiteren Ablauf heraushalten und insbesondere keine Planänderungen fordern, jedenfalls keine nicht durchkalkulierten und in ihrer Konsequenz nicht überschaubaren. Der Aufsichtsrat muss mehrheitlich mit Fachleuten, nicht mit Baulaien aus der Politik besetzt sein. Schließlich sind auch Transparenz und Öffentlichkeit im Verfahren für das Gelingen unerlässlich.

„Die Politik als Bauherr hat versagt", solche Schlagzeilen müssen doch künftig vermieden werden können.

May 23, 2012, the Chairman of the Supervisory Board, Berlin's Governing Mayor Klaus Wowereit, announced the dismissal of the design team, acting in his habitual mode of the doer, the one who takes charge of things.

The consequences of this decision were immediately clear to all professionals, and even to other observers. The MCA (maximum credible accident) became an ultimate MCA. The dismissal of the entire team with its knowledge base was to cost several years in extra time and hundreds of millions of additional euros. It seemed as if, except for a bit of touching-up, the architects had really done their design work, and what remained to be done was just bring some security and fire safety installations up to standard. Therefore, many people thought that the delay would be no more than a few months, or a year at the most. However, the technical problems turned out to be serious. This meant that teams new to the project had to be brought on board, without binding contracts, with remuneration based on time spent. These teams took several months to work their way into this complex project and also tried to shed light on the undocumented and uncontrolled growth by carrying out a survey. Owing to the various modifications, the smoke extraction system had become so complicated that it was beyond manageable control. Cable ducts carried the wrong cables and were over-loaded; fire compartment boundaries were thoughtlessly penetrated; and uncertified building components had been fitted. The software of the security installations was not up to the task. A huge gap remained before one could hope to obtain permission to operate. Many installations were dismantled and reinstalled, some even twice.

In retrospect it is clear that, in 2012, a radical solution would have been quicker and cheaper: stripping out, producing new designs, and the installation of new services for the entire terminal rather than redesign and reconstruction. Instead, several successors to the failed managing director and several CTOs, as well as numerous design companies, external consultants and controllers, tried to get a grip on the project. They all failed due to the fact that there were no longer any reliable plans and it was therefore impossible to engage companies on the basis of binding contracts with fixed deadlines and agreed prices. The companies were only prepared to work upon instruction and on an hourly basis spent, i.e., at no risk—with the inevitable consequences for costs and deadlines.

Finally, the new Chairman of the Management Board, Engelbert Lütke Daldrup, who was appointed in 2017, was able to put the project back on a solid footing. He suc-ceeded in committing all protagonists—who up until then had worked against each other, rather than collaborate—to the same cause and in bringing order to the design and, above all, to the contractual procedure.

No new opening date was announced. First, it was necessary to establish sufficient certainty before the announcement was made: the first plane will land on October 31, 2020, as scheduled but with an eight-year delay.

The fact that Lütke Daldrup saw no good reason for major celebrations and quietly handed over the new airport to its operators was understandable in view of the endless sequence of mistakes, failures, scandals, and the financial disaster. The fact that the opening date happened to be overshadowed by the Coronavirus pandemic, and therefore air traffic was very slow to pick up, was positive because it was possible to attune all the operating systems without stress.

Now that the air has cleared, the new airport can finally demonstrate its functional advantages in operation, and perhaps it will even be possible to judge its architecture without prejudice. Even though, architecturally speaking, the building project has been successfully completed, the long-term funding of Flughafengesellschaft is far from cut and dried owing to the mountain of debts.

The question as to what society can learn for future mega-projects, what one could have done better and right, is not easy to answer owing to the multifaceted nature of the failures. Perhaps this much can be said: the project must be professionally planned and designed in depth, and it must be possible to calculate realistic costs before making a political decision authorizing the building project together with a budget. The role of the client must be played by professionals, for example a high-profile consortium with international expertise that must guarantee costs and deadlines. Politicians must keep out of the ongoing process and, in particular, must not stipulate any changes to the plan, at least not any changes the costs of which have not been calculated and the consequences of which are not predictable. The majority of the supervisory board members must be professionals rather than politicians who are lay people in terms of construction. Finally, for success it is indispensable that the process be transparent and open.

"The Failure of Politicians as Clients"; it should really be possible to avoid such headlines in the future!

Dokumentation
Documentation

1   Zugangskontrollstelle West
     Access control point west
2   Betriebstankstelle West
     Operational fueling station west
3   Winterdienst
     Winter services
4   Feuerwache West
     Fire station west
5   Spezialgeräteservice/Werkstatt
     Special equipment service/workshop
6   Terminal 1
     Terminal 1
7   Nordpier
     North pier
8   Südpier
     South pier
9   Feuerwache Ost
     Fire station east
10   Betriebstankstelle Ost
     Operational fueling station east
11   Zugangskontrollstelle Ost
     Access control point east
12   Technische Instandhaltung
     Technical maintenance center
13   Abfallwirtschaft Ost
     Waste collection point

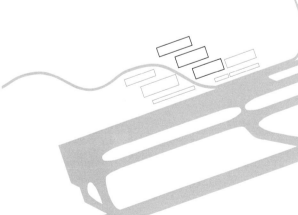

◇   realisiert
    built
◇   nicht realisiert
    not built

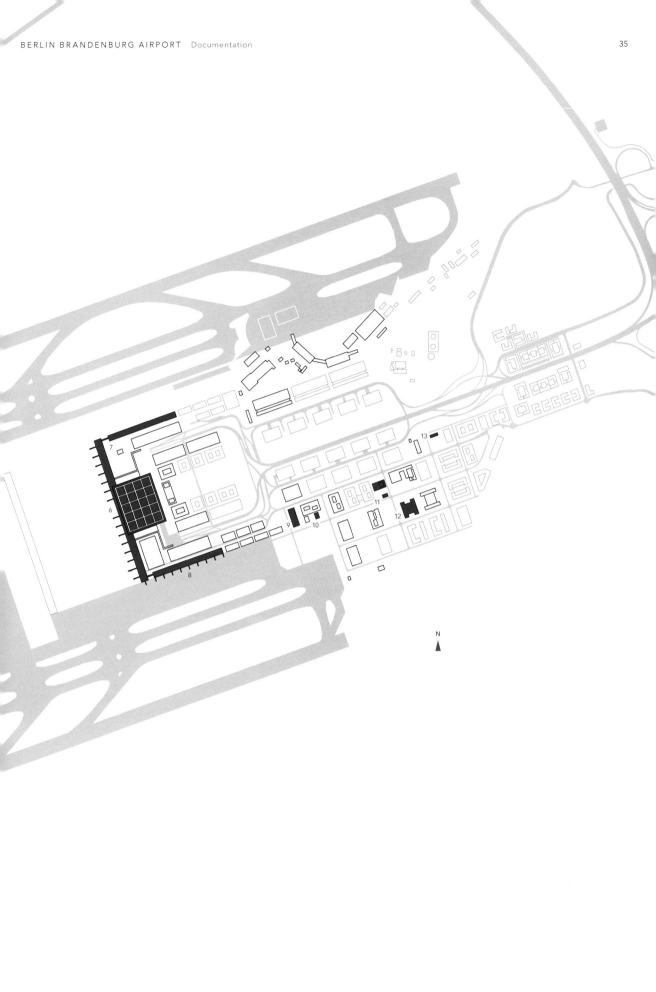

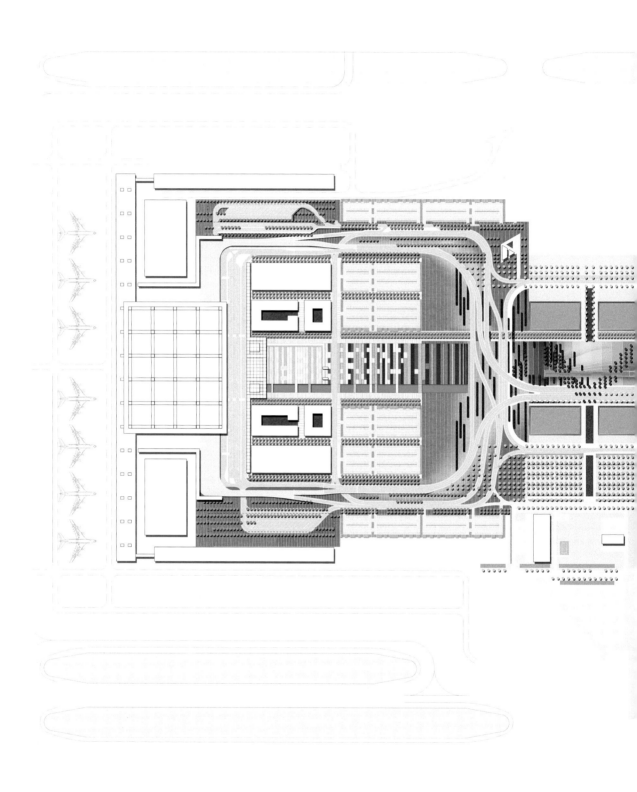

↗   Freiraumkonzept
Open-space design

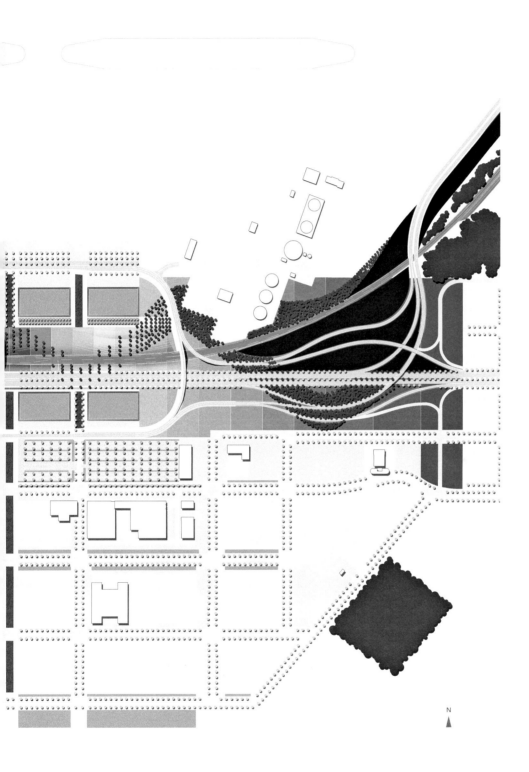

Ein durchgängiges Freiraumkonzept moduliert die eiszeitlich geprägte brandenburgisch-märkische Kulturlandschaft ab dem Eingang zum Flughafengelände im Osten zu einer urbanen Landschaft im Bereich der Airport City im Zentrum, wo die Freiflächen durch Hecken, geometrisch geordnete Haine und Alleen strukturiert sind.

A consistent open-space design shapes the cultivated Brandenburg landscape (Märkische Landschaft) from the entrance to the air-port grounds in the east into an urban landscape in the Airport City area at the center, where the open areas are structured by hedges, geometrically arranged groves, and avenues.

Funktionales und gestalterisches Städtebaukonzept

Eine Besonderheit des Flughafens Berlin Brandenburg besteht darin, dass all seine Gebäude einem übergeordneten, gemeinsamen Gestaltungscodex unterliegen, der von gmp entwickelt wurde. Dieses „Gestaltungshandbuch" stellt, auch im Rahmen künftiger Entwicklungen – etwa bei einem Ausbau der Passagierkapazitäten –, die Kontinuität in der Gestaltung sicher. Für alle planenden Disziplinen verbindliche Gestaltungsgrundsätze sind im Handbuch festgeschrieben – für alle Maßstabsebenen, von der städtebaulichen Entwicklung über die Hauptachsen und Maßsysteme bis hin zu Gebäudekubaturen, Materialien, Farben und Möblierung.

Maßgeblich für den Entwurf ist ein horizontales Grundraster von 6,25 Metern, das sich ableitet aus der Breite von Flugzeugen der Kategorie C (z. B. Boeing 737 oder Airbus A320) von 37 bis 42 Metern (A), dem durchschnittlichen Abstand der Check-in-Inseln von 43,75 Metern (B) und dem optimalen Stützenabstand in der Gepäckförderanlage von 12,5 Metern (C). Multipliziert mit 7 ergibt sich aus dem Hauptmodul von 6,25 Metern das Großmodul von 43,75 Metern. Das Nebenraster ist im Verhältnis zum Hauptraster um die Hälfte, also 3,125 Meter, versetzt angelegt. Das Hauptmodul durch 5 geteilt ergibt das Grundmodul von 1,25 Metern. Dieses Raster durchzieht den Flughafen von der Großform bis zur Teilung des Natursteinbodens.

Als Grundmaß für das vertikale Raster, an dem sich alle Aufrisse und Schnitte orientieren, wurden 1,30 Meter festgelegt. Auch diese Maßordnung gilt für alle Bauteile von den Gebäudehöhen in der Silhouette bis zum Schaltertresen.

Functional and Conceptual Urban Design Concept

A special feature of Berlin Brandenburg Airport is that all its buildings are based on a general shared design code developed by gmp. This Design Manual ensures the continuity of the design also for future developments, such as those needed to increase passenger capacity. The Manual specifies mandatory design principles for all planning disciplines and scales, from urban design development to main axes and dimensional systems through to building volumes, materials, colors, and furniture.

A key element of the design is the basic horizontal grid of 6.25 meters which, multiplied by 7, results in the primary grid, which in turn is derived from the width of category C airplanes (e.g. Boeing 737 or Airbus A320) of between 37 and 42 meters (A) and the average distance between check-in islands of 43.75 meters (B); the optimal column spacing for the baggage conveyor system of 12.5 meters (C) is twice the basic grid. Thus the primary grid is 43.75 meters; the secondary grid is offset by half of the basic grid dimension, i.e., by 3.125 meters. Dividing the or basic grid by five results in the basic module of 1.25 meters. This grid dimension is used throughout the airport, from large building elements down to the joints of the natural stone floor.

For the vertical grid a basic dimension of 1.30 meters was determined, which is used in all elevations and sections. Again, this dimensional order applies to all parts and components of the building, from the overall height down to the height of counters.

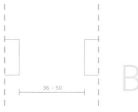

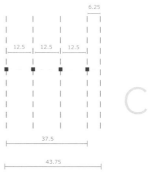

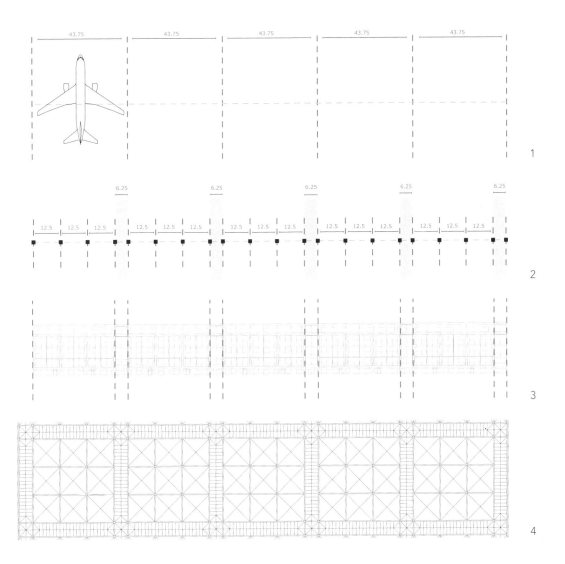

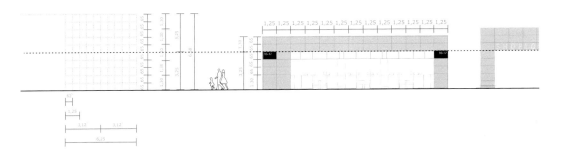

↑ Horizontales (oben) und vertikales (unten) Grundraster
Horizontal (top) and vertical (bottom) basic grid

1 Primärraster
Primary grid
2 Bandraster
Basic grid
3 Bandraster Fassade
Basic grid, facade
4 Bandraster Dach
Basic grid, roof

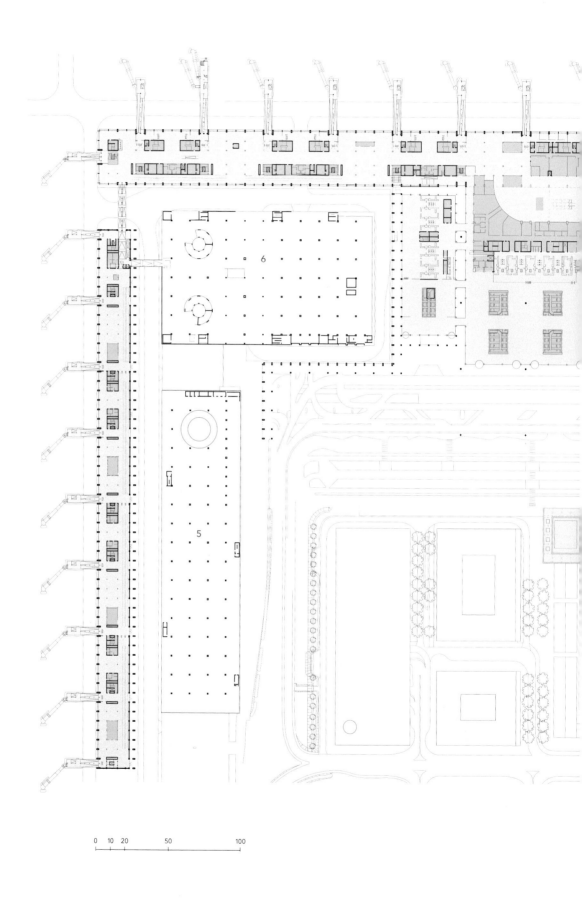

Grundriss Terminalgebäude, Abflugebene 1
Floor plan of departure level 1, terminal building

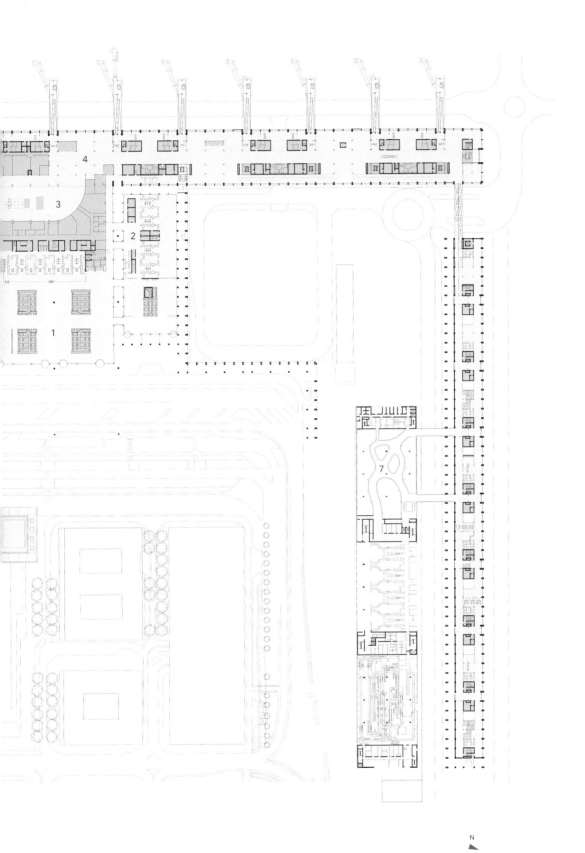

1   Check-in-Halle
    Check-in hall
2   Sicherheitskontrolle
    Security area
3   Marktplatz
    Marketplace
4   Abflugebene Schengen
    Departure level (Schengen)
5   Parken
    Parking
6   VIP-Parken
    VIP parking
7   Terminal 2
    (Entwurf: ATP)
    Terminal 2
    (design: ATP)

Grundriss Abflugebene 2
Floor plan of departure level 2

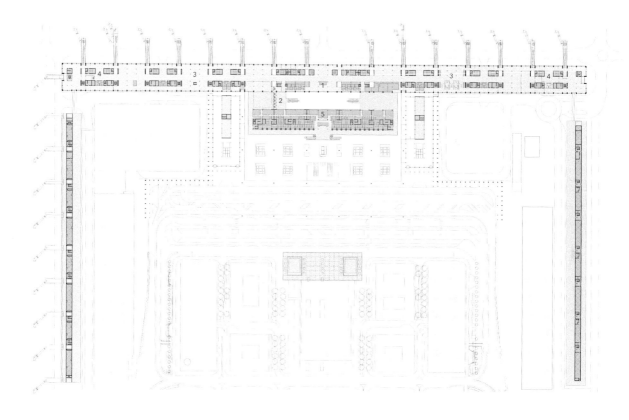

0   20   50   100

1   Sicherheitskontrolle
    Security area
2   Ausreisekontrollen
    Exit checks
3   Abflug Non-Schengen
    Non-Schengen departure
4   Airline-Lounges
    Airline lounges
5   Raum der Stille
    Room of Silence

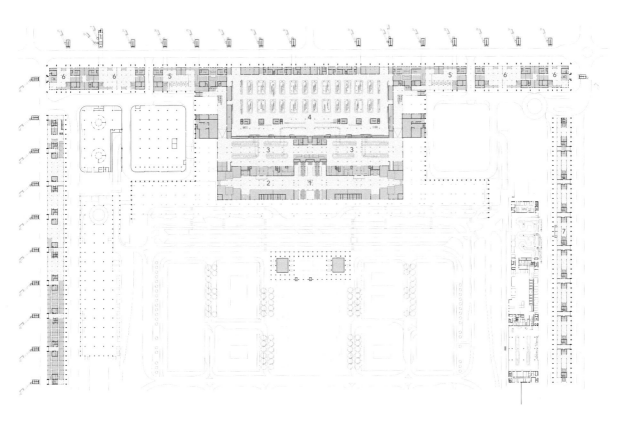

Grundriss Ankunftsebene
Floor plan of arrival level

1 Zugang Bahnhof
Entrance to/from railway station
2 Ankunftshalle
Arrival hall
3 Gepäckausgabe
Baggage claim
4 Gepäcksortierung
Baggage sorting
5 Einreisekontrollen
Entry checks
6 Busgates
Bus gates
7 Walkboarding
Walk-boarding

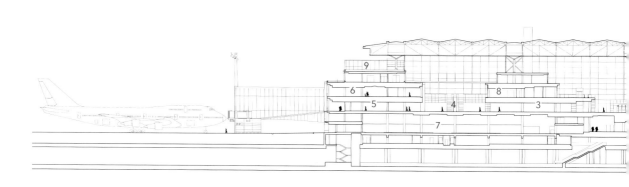

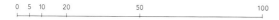

0 5 10   20   50   100

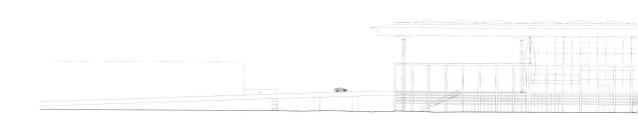

↑   Längsschnitte
Longitudinal sections

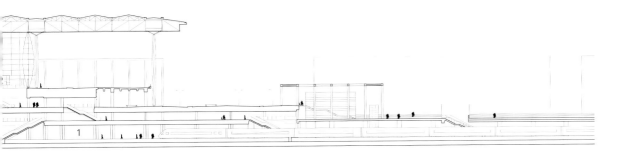

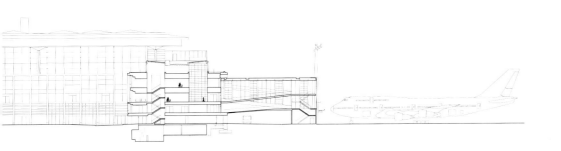

1 Bahnhof
   Railway station
2 Check-in-Halle
   Check-in hall
3 Sicherheitskontrolle
   Security area
4 Marktplatz
   Marketplace
5 Abflugebene Schengen
   Departure level (Schengen)
6 Abflugebene Non-Schengen
   Departure level (Non-Schengen)
7 Gepäcksortierung
   Baggage sorting
8 Raum der Stille
   Room of Silence
9 Besucherterrasse
   Observation deck

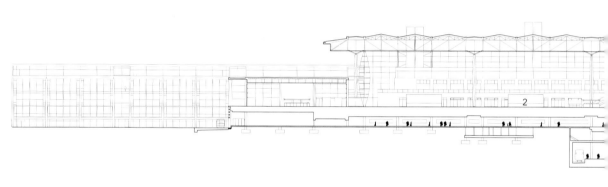

0 5 10   20   50   100

↑ Querschnitt
Cross section

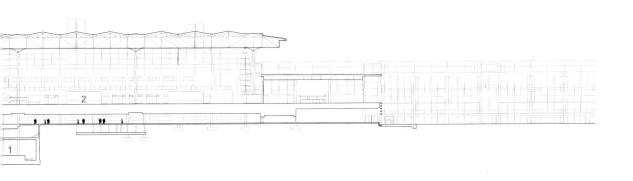

1   Bahnhof
    Railway station
2   Check-in-Halle
    Check-in hall

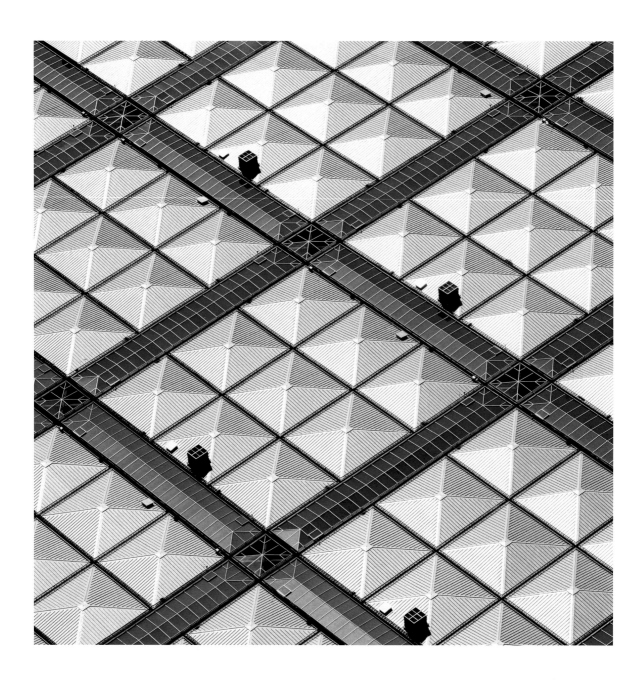

⊡← Vorfahrt Terminalgebäude
Terminal building, drop-off area

↑   Dachaufsicht Check-in-Halle
Aerial view of the check-in hall roof

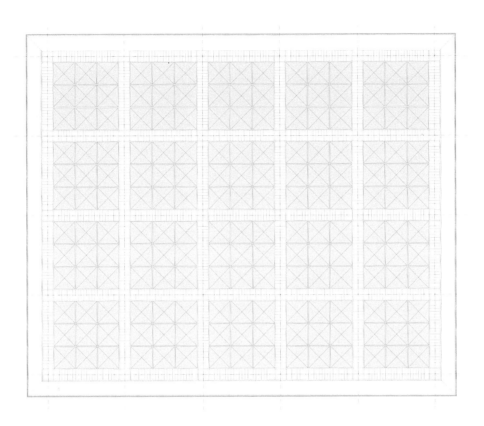

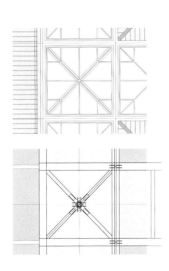

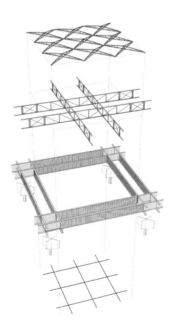

↑ Detail Stützenkopf/Dach, Aufsicht
Detail of head of column/roof,
top view
Detail Stützenkopf/Dach, Untersicht
Detail of head of column/roof,
bottom view

↑ Dachaufsicht
Plan view of the roof

1 Tertiärtragwerk
Tertiary structure
2 Sekundärtragwerk
Secondary structure
3 Primärtragwerk
Primary structure
4 Tertiärtragwerk
Tertiary structure

Zugang zur Check-in-Halle mit Installation
THE Magic Carpet von Pae White
Access to check-in hall featuring the installation
THE Magic Carpet by Pae White

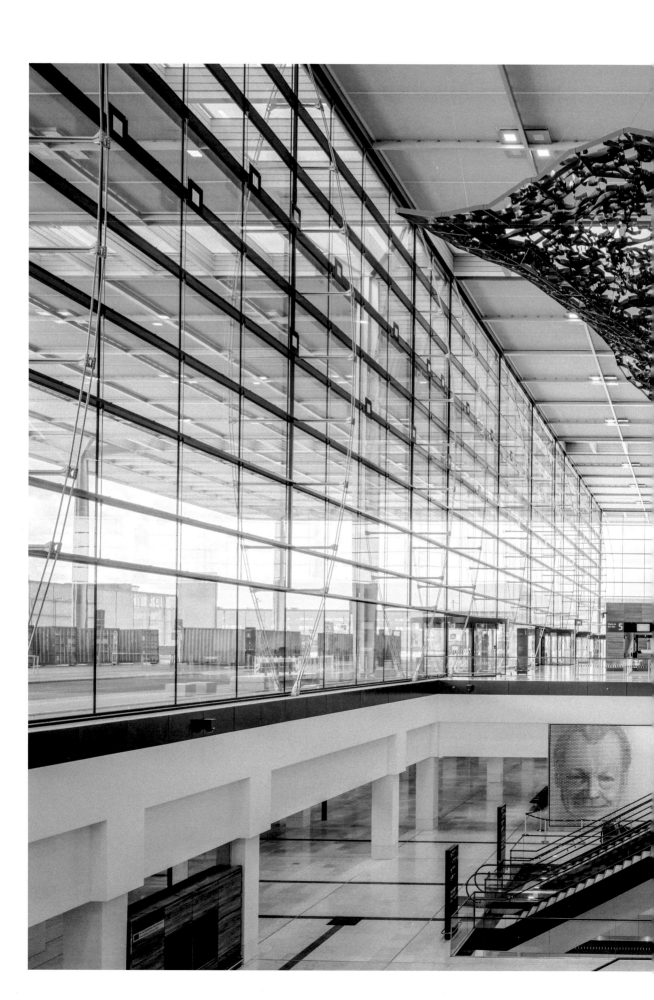

Terminalhalle mit Check-in-Schaltern und Sicherheitskontrollen
Terminal hall with check-in desks and security controls

Das Leitsystem

Internationale Flughäfen, die sich aufgrund ihrer Dimension und Komplexität meist nicht auf einen Blick erfassen lassen, benötigen ein Leitsystem, das die Orientierung rasch und unmissverständlich ermöglicht und sich Reisenden verschiedenster Sprachen und Kulturkreise erschließt.

Das vom Büro für Kommunikationsdesign Moniteurs in enger Zusammenarbeit mit gmp entwickelte Grafikdesign des Leit- und Orientierungssystems für das gesamte Areal des Flughafens Berlin Brandenburg setzt sich im Wesentlichen aus drei Elementen zusammen: einer Familie von Piktogrammen, einer Schriftfamilie und einem Farbkonzept. Das Wegeleitsystem ist eingebunden in das Architekturraster, das der Gestaltung des Fluggastterminals zugrunde liegt: Größe und Platzierung der Beschilderungen leiten sich aus diesem Raster ab.

Leitidee ist die Übersetzung der geradlinigen Architektursprache in lineare grafische Strukturen. Grundfarbe ist ein dunkles Rot für die Fluginformationen, besetzt mit weißer Schrift, womit Assoziationen an die Landesfarben von Berlin und Brandenburg geweckt werden. Das Rot taucht in der Architektur nirgends als eigenständige Farbe auf und ist daher auf den Schildern unauffällig präsent. Es hat einen hohen Wiedererkennungswert, ebenso wie die Hausschrift BER Signage mit der zugehörigen Piktogramm-Familie. Konstruktive Elemente des Leitsystems und Serviceinformationen erscheinen wie die konstruktiven architektonischen Elemente in einem dunklen Grau. Deutsche und englische Beschriftungen unterscheiden sich durch Schriftgröße und Schriftschnitt voneinander.

The Guidance System

Owing to size and complexity, the layout of international airports cannot be grasped just by looking at the building and interior features, which means that a guidance system that helps travelers find their way quickly and clearly and that can be understood by people from other parts of the world is needed.

The graphic design of the guidance and orientation system for the entire Berlin Brandenburg Airport was developed by Moniteurs, Communication Design Consultants, in close cooperation with gmp and essentially comprises three elements: a family of pictograms, a family of fonts, and a color concept. The guidance system is also governed by the architectural grid that underlies the passenger terminal: the size and placing of the signage is based on this grid.

The basic idea is to translate the straight architectural form into linear graphic structures. The basic color is a deep red with white lettering, which is used for flight information; the color also evokes associations with the Berlin and Brandenburg state colors. Red is not used as an independent color elsewhere in the architecture, which gives the signage a distinct appearance that can be easily recognized, just like the bespoke corporate font BER Signage and its associated pictogram family. Structural elements of the guidance system and service information are designed in dark gray, just like the structural architectural elements. The German and English lettering is differentiated by size and font style.

↗ Wegeleitsystem im Terminal
   und im Außengelände
   Guidance system in the terminal
   and outdoor areas

⊡← Marktplatz im Abflugbereich mit Shopping- und Gastronomieangeboten   ↑   Hauptpier
Marketplace in the departure area with shops, restaurants and cafés   Main pier

↑ Zugang zu den Gates
   Access to the gates

Abflugwartebereich mit Blick auf das Vorfeld
Waiting area with a view of the apron

Gläserne Fluggastbrücken
Glass jetways

Blick vom Vorfeld auf den Hauptpier
Main pier as seen from the apron

⊡← Luftseite, Terminalgebäude und Hauptpier   ←↑ Südpier
Airside, terminal building and main pier   South pier

Gepäckabfertigung
Baggage handling

Gepäckausgabe
Baggage claim hall

Ankunftsbereich unter der Terminalhalle
Arrival area beneath the terminal building

Service-Gebäude für den Flughafenbetrieb

Zu den Betriebsgebäuden im peripheren Bereich des Flughafens, die gmp realisiert hat, gehören neben dem Stützpunkt für Technische Instandhaltung mit dem Rechenzentrum, der Abfallsammelstelle, der Winterdiensthalle, den Zugangskontrollen West und Ost und den Betriebstankstellen West und Ost zwei der drei Feuerwehrstandorte.

Die Feuerwache West auf dem Gelände der Maintenance City westlich des Vorfelds beherbergt neben den Räumen der Feuerwehr, den beiden Hallen für Großfahrzeuge und der Feuerwehrleitstelle das Airport Control Center, die Notfalleinsatzzentrale, die Sicherheitsleitstelle und die Leitstelle Technik. Die Feuerwache Ost in der Service City südöstlich des Hauptterminals umfasst drei Fahrzeughallen mit 14 Stellplätzen für Einsatzfahrzeuge und ist neben der Brandabwehr beim Flugbetrieb in erster Linie dem Gebäudebrandschutz des Terminals verpflichtet.

Vor Fassaden – und Fenstern – liegt eine Membran, die der Radardämmung dient, die Radarüberwachung jedoch nicht beeinträchtigt und trotzdem von innen den vollen Durchblick von den Kontrollräumen auf das Vorfeld erlaubt. Gleichzeitig schützt sie vor Sonneneinstrahlung und Überhitzung, da sie als außen liegende, zweite Fassade einen Kamineffekt erzeugt und so zur Kühlung beiträgt.

Alle Betriebsgebäude von gmp wurden auf der Basis des Gestaltungshandbuches entworfen und zeigen die typische Horizontalgliederung.

Service Buildings for Airport Operations

The service buildings at the periphery of the airport designed by gmp include two of the three fire stations in addition to the technical maintenance center with computer center, the waste collection point, the winter services hall, the access control points west and est, and the operational fueling stations west and east.

Fire Station West is part of the Maintenance City to the west of the apron and includes the facilities of the fire brigade, the two halls for large vehicles, and the fire brigade control center, as well as the Airport Control Center, the emergency services center, the security control center, and the technical control center. Fire Station East at the Service City to the south-east of the main terminal comprises two vehicle halls with 14 parking spaces for emergency vehicles and is primarily responsible for fire protection of the terminal building and aircraft-related fire incidents.

A radar-shielding membrane is fitted in front of facades and windows that does not interfere with radar monitoring but nevertheless permits unimpeded views from the control rooms to the apron. At the same time, the membrane protects against solar irradiation and overheating because, as a second outside "skin," it causes a chimney effect in the gap that contributes to cooling the building.

All service buildings by gmp were designed on the basis of the Design Manual, including the typical horizontal grid structure.

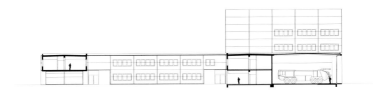

0   5   10   20

↗   Schnitt
    Section

Feuerwache West in der Maintenance City
Fire Station West at the Maintenance City

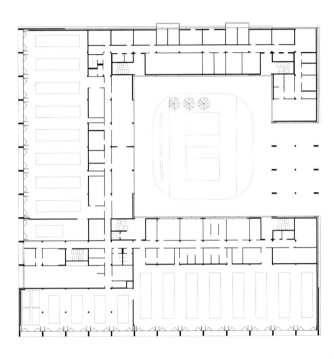

```
0    5    10        20
```

N

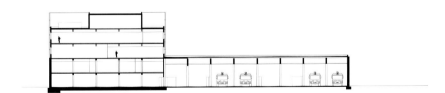

↑ Grundriss Erdgeschoss   ↑ Schnitt
   Ground floor plan   Section

Fahrzeughalle
Vehicle hall

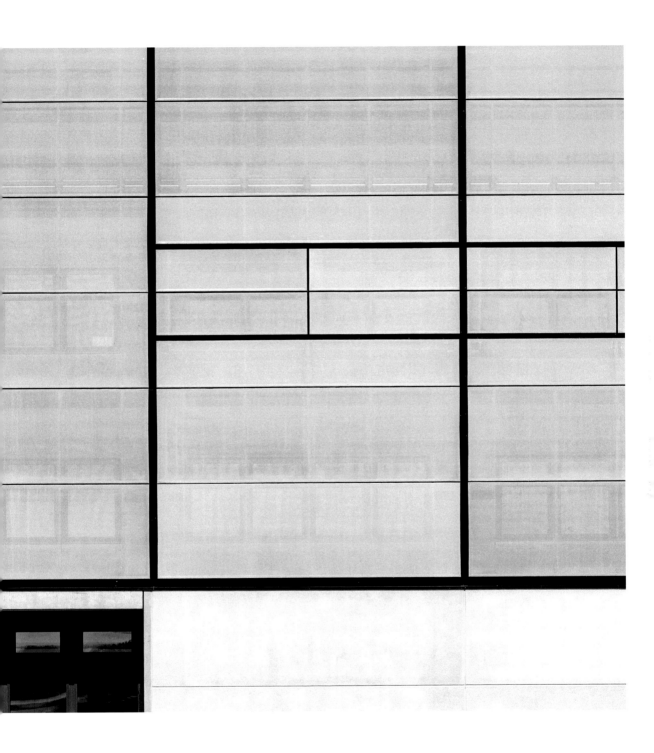

Membranfassade mit charakteristischer Horizontalgliederung
Membrane facade with characteristic horizontal structure

↑ ↗   Betriebstankstelle Ost
Operational fueling station east

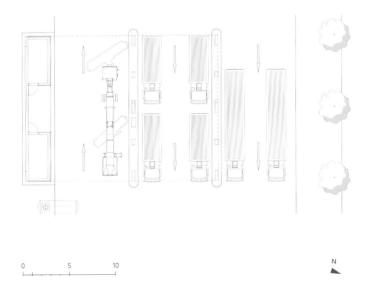

0   5   10

N

↗ Grundriss Betriebstankstelle Ost
   Floor plan of operational fueling station east

Raum der Stille

Im Zentrum von Terminal 1, auf Ebene E2 in der Mittelachse, zugänglich von der Abflughalle aus, bietet der Raum der Stille einen Rückzugsort für Menschen verschiedener Kulturen und Religionen, der den hektischen Betrieb des Flughafens vergessen lässt.

Die Abgeschiedenheit wird durch eine Sequenz von Vorräumen erreicht. Zwei Eingänge führen in einen Quergang, in dessen Mittelachse sich ein kleiner quadratischer Vorraum mit dem mehrsprachigen skulpturalen Schriftzug „Stille" anschließt, von dem aus man zur Linken über einen weiteren quadratischen Vorraum in den überkonfessionellen Raum, zur Rechten auf gleiche Weise in die christliche Kapelle gelangt.

So stehen der bekenntnisunabhängige und der christliche Andachtsraum gleichwertig nebeneinander, unterschieden nur durch die liturgische Ausstattung.

Böden, Wände und gestufte Decken der Räume bestehen aus groben, gebrannten Ziegeln. Horizontale Lichtfugen sorgen für eine kontemplative Atmosphäre. Das Oculus im Zenit der abgetreppten Decken ist gleichfalls indirekt beleuchtet und öffnet den Raum gen Himmel.

Room of Silence

At the center of Terminal 1, on level E2 in the central axis and accessible from the departure hall, the Room of Silence is a place to which people of different cultures and religions can retreat, leaving the hectic airport activities behind them.

Its seclusion is achieved by a sequence of ante-rooms. Two entrances lead to a transverse corridor and from there—in its central axis—to a small square ante-room with the multilingual sculptural inscription "Silence"; from here, to the left, one reaches the nondenominational prayer room via a further square ante-room and, to the right, the Christian chapel, also via such an anteroom.

In this way, the nondenominational and Christian prayer rooms are given equal importance and differ only in their liturgical fixtures.

The floors, walls, and stepped ceilings of the rooms consist of coarse fired bricks. Horizontal strips of light create an atmosphere conducive to contemplation. The oculus at the zenith of each of the stepped ceilings is also lit indirectly and opens the space towards the sky.

0 1   5   10

← Raumsequenz im Eingangsbereich
  Sequence of rooms as seen in the entrance area

↑ Schnitt durch den Eingangsbereich (oben),
  Schnitt durch die Andachtsräume (unten)
  Section through the entrance area (top);
  section through the prayer rooms (bottom)

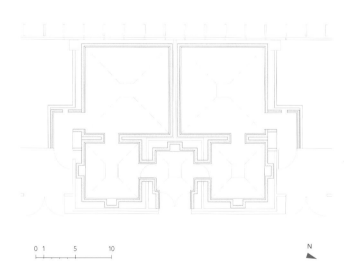

0 1   5   10

N

↑→   Andachtsräume
     Prayer rooms

↑   Grundriss
    Floor plan

Anhang
Appendix

gmp-Entwurfsteam
gmp Design Team

Meinhard von Gerkan
Prof. Dr. h. c. mult. Dipl.-Ing. Architekt BDA

geboren 1935 in Riga, Lettland. Gemeinsam mit Volkwin Marg gründete Meinhard von Gerkan 1965 gmp · Architekten von Gerkan, Marg und Partner. Von 1974 bis 2002 hatte von Gerkan den Lehrstuhl für Entwerfen an der Technischen Universität Braunschweig inne, 2002 verlieh ihm die Philipps-Universität Marburg, 2005 die Chung Yuan Christian University die Ehrendoktorwürde. 2007 ernannte die School of Design der East China Normal University in Shanghai von Gerkan zum Ehrenprofessor, seit 2014 ist er Advising Professor der Tongji University in Shanghai. Von Gerkan ist Mitbegründer der gmp-Stiftung und der Academy for Architectural Culture (aac) und hat zahlreiche Auszeichnungen erhalten, darunter den Rumänischen Staatspreis, den Großen Preis des Bundes Deutscher Architekten, das Bundesverdienstkreuz 1. Klasse und den Liang-Sicheng-Preis der Architectural Society of China. Zu seinen bekanntesten Projekten zählen der Flughafen Berlin-Tegel, der Berliner Hauptbahnhof, die Villa Guna im lettischen Jūrmala, das Hanoi Museum, das Grand Theater in Chongqing, der Neu- und Umbau des Chinesischen Nationalmuseums in Peking und die Planung der Stadt Lingang New City (heute Nanhui New City) bei Shanghai.

Born in 1935 in Riga, Latvia. In 1965, together with Volkwin Marg, Meinhard von Gerkan founded gmp · von Gerkan, Marg and Partners Architects. From 1974 to 2002, von Gerkan held the Chair of Architectural Design at the Technical University of Braunschweig. He was awarded an honorary doctorate by Philipps University of Marburg in 2002 and also by Chung Yuan Christian University in 2005. In 2007, the School of Design of East China Normal University in Shanghai awarded von Gerkan an honorary professorship and, since 2014, he has been Advising Professor at Tongji University in Shanghai. Von Gerkan is a co-founder of the gmp Foundation and the Academy for Architectural Culture (aac). He has received numerous awards, including the Romanian State Prize, the Grand Award of the Association of German Architects (BDA), the Federal Cross of Merit, First Class, and the Liang Sicheng Prize of the Architectural Society of China. His best known projects include Berlin-Tegel Airport, Berlin Main Railway Station, Villa Guna in Jūrmala, Latvia, the Hanoi Museum, the Grand Theater in Chongqing, the reconstruction and renovation of the National Museum of China in Beijing, and the master plan of Lingang New City (today Nanhui New City) near Shanghai.

Hubert Nienhoff
Dipl.-Ing. Architekt

geboren 1959 in Kirchhellen. Nach seinem Diplom an der RWTH Aachen war Nienhoff zunächst für Christoph Mäckler Architekten tätig. 1988 bis 1991 war er Assistent am Lehrstuhl für Stadtbereichsplanung und Werklehre der RWTH Aachen und kam 1988 zu gmp · Architekten von Gerkan, Marg und Partner, wo er seit 1993 Partner ist. Zu den von ihm verantworteten Projekten zählen unter anderem die Neue Messe Leipzig, der Bahnhof Berlin-Spandau, das Olympiastadion Berlin, WM-Stadien in Südafrika und Brasilien, das Hans-Sachs-Haus in Gelsenkirchen sowie die Neue Messe Teheran. Als Mitinitiator der aac (Academy for Architectural Culture) engagiert er sich für die Förderung junger Architektinnen und Architekten.

Born in 1959 in Kirchhellen, Germany. After qualifying at RWTH Aachen University, Nienhoff started working for Christoph Mäckler Architects. From 1988 to 1991, he was assistant professor at the Chair of Urban Design and Material Studies at RWTH Aachen University and, in 1988, joined gmp · von Gerkan, Marg and Partners Architects where he was appointed partner in 1993. The projects for which he has been responsible include the New Leipzig Trade Fair Center, the Berlin Spandau Railway Station, the Berlin Olympic Stadium, World Cup stadiums in South Africa and Brazil, the Hans-Sachs-Haus in Gelsenkirchen, and the New Exhibition Center in Tehran. As one of the initiators of the Academy for Architectural Culture (aac), he is involved in the advancement of young architects.

Hans Joachim Paap
Dipl.-Ing. (FH) Architekt BDA

geboren 1960 in Braunschweig. Nach Abschluss seines Architekturstudiums an der Technischen Universität Braunschweig war er von 1995 bis 2001 als wissenschaftlicher Mitarbeiter am dortigen Institut für Baugestaltung bei Meinhard von Gerkan tätig. 1997 kam er zu gmp · Architekten von Gerkan, Marg und Partner, wo er seit 2009 assoziierter Partner ist. Paap ist Vorsitzender der Hans Schaefers Stiftung und stellvertretender Vorsitzender des Berliner Landesverbandes des Bundes Deutscher Architektinnen und Architekten (BDA). Unter seiner Leitung entstanden bei gmp Projekte wie die Commerzbank-Arena in Frankfurt am Main oder die Erweiterung des Flughafens Lübeck. Aktuell wird in Berlin das Quartier Heidestraße „The Crown" realisiert.

Born in 1960 in Braunschweig, Germany. After completing his diploma course in architecture at Braunschweig Technical University, he joined the scientific staff at the Institute for Building Design under Meinhard von Gerkan, where he worked from 1995 until 2001. In 1997, he joined gmp · von Gerkan, Marg and Partners Architects and was appointed associate partner in 2009. Paap is chairman of the Hans Schaefers Foundation and deputy chairman of the Berlin branch of the Association of German Architects (BDA). At gmp, he was responsible for projects such as the Commerzbank Arena in Frankfurt am Main and the extension of Lübeck Airport; currently, he is working on The Crown Quarter on Heidestrasse, Berlin.

Jochen Köhn
Dipl.-Ing. Architekt

geboren 1964 in Hamburg. Köhn studierte Architektur an der RWTH Aachen und kam 1994 zu gmp · Architekten von Gerkan, Marg und Partner; seit 2010 ist er assoziierter Partner und Mitglied der erweiterten Geschäftsführung. Als Office Manager am Standort Berlin ist Köhn für Vertragsgestaltung, Honorare und Personalentwicklung zuständig. Als Projektleiter war er unter anderem an der Realisierung von Großprojekten wie der Neuen Messe Leipzig, der Sanierung und Modernisierung des Berliner Olympiastadions sowie den WM-Stadien in Südafrika, Brasilien und Russland beteiligt.

Born in 1964 in Hamburg, Germany. Köhn studied architecture at RWTH Aachen Technical University and, in 1994, joined gmp · von Gerkan, Marg and Partners Architects; he was appointed associate partner in 2010 and is a member of the extended company management. As office manager at the Berlin branch, Köhn is responsible for contract management, fees, and human resources development. In his role as project leader he was involved in large projects such as the New Leipzig Trade Fair Center, the World Cup stadiums in South Africa, Brazil, and Russia, as well as the refurbishment and modernization of the Berlin Olympic Stadium.

Autoren und Fotografen
Authors and Photographers

Jürgen Tietz
Dr., Architekturkritiker und Publizist
Architecture critic and publicist

studierte Kunstgeschichte, Klassische Archäologie sowie Ur- und Frühgeschichte und arbeitet als Publizist und Moderator zu den Themen Architektur und Denkmalpflege. Er schreibt für Fachzeitschriften und Tageszeitungen und ist Autor zahlreicher Bücher, zuletzt erschienen *Drei Monde der Moderne oder wie die Moderne klassisch wurde* (2019) und *TXL. Berlin Tegel Airport* (2020). Tietz ist Mitglied im Gestaltungsbeirat der Stadt Fulda, stellvertretender Vorsitzender des Hochhausbeirats Düsseldorf und engagiert sich in der Arbeitsgruppe Öffentlichkeitsarbeit des Deutschen Nationalkomitees für Denkmalschutz.

Jürgen Tietz studied art history, classical archaeology, pre- and early history. He works as a publicist and moderator of discussions on architecture and monument preservation. He writes for professional journals and daily newspapers and has authored numerous books, including his most recent publications *Drei Monde der Moderne oder wie die Moderne klassisch wurde* (2019) and *TXL. Berlin Tegel Airport* (2020). Tietz is a member of the design advisory board for the City of Fulda, deputy chair of the advisory board for high-rise buildings in Düsseldorf, and a member of the public relations working group of the German National Committee for the Protection of Monuments.

Falk Jaeger
Prof. Dr., Autor und Journalist
Author and journalist

studierte Architektur und Kunstgeschichte in Braunschweig, Stuttgart und Tübingen und wurde an der TU Hannover promoviert. Seit 1976 arbeitet er als freier Architekturkritiker. 1983 bis 1988 war er Assistent am Institut für Baugeschichte und Bauaufnahme der TU Berlin. Jaeger lehrte an verschiedenen Hochschulen und hatte von 1993 bis 2000 den Lehrstuhl für Architekturtheorie an der TU Dresden inne. Jaeger lebt als freier Publizist, Dozent, Kurator und Fachjournalist in Berlin.

Falk Jaeger studied architecture and art history in Braunschweig, Stuttgart, and Tübingen, and was awarded a doctorate by the Technical University Hanover. He has been working as an independent architectural critic since 1976. From 1983 to 1988, he worked as assistant at the Department for Architectural History and Building Surveying at TU Berlin. Jaeger taught at several universities, and from 1993 to 2000 he was chair of the Department of Architectural Theory at TU Dresden. Jaeger lives in Berlin and works as an independent publicist, associate professor, curator, and journalist.

Leit- und Orientierungssystem
Guidance and Orientation System

Marcus Bredt
Fotograf
Photographer

Moniteurs – Sibylle Schlaich und Heike Nehl
Dipl.-Designerinnen

wurde von 1992 bis 1994 am Lette-Verein in Berlin zum Fotografen ausgebildet. Er spezialisierte sich früh auf Architekturfotografie und arbeitet für internationale Auftraggeber wie Daniel Libeskind oder Sauerbruch Hutton. Bredt begleitet gmp seit 2004 weltweit mit seinen Aufnahmen. Er hat zahlreiche nationale Projekte wie den Berliner Hauptbahnhof ebenso dokumentiert wie internationale, etwa in China, Vietnam, Südafrika oder Brasilien.

Marcus Bredt was educated as a photographer at the Lette-Verein in Berlin between 1992 and 1994. Early on, he specialized in architectural photography and worked with international architects such as Daniel Libeskind and Sauerbruch Hutton. Since 2004, Bredt has photographed the works of gmp all over the world. He has documented several projects, both nationally—such as Berlin's Central Station, and internationally—throughout China, Vietnam, South Africa, and Brazil.

Sibylle Schlaich studierte visuelle Kommunikation an der Hochschule der Künste in Berlin und an der HfG – Hochschule für Gestaltung Schwäbisch Gmünd. Heike Nehl studierte visuelle Kommunikation an der FH Bielefeld University of Applied Sciences. Gemeinsam mit Heidi Specker gründeten beide 1994 Moniteurs Kommunikationsdesign mit einem Fokus auf Informationsdesign und Wegeleitsysteme. Zu den wichtigsten Projekten von Moniteurs zählen der Flughafen München, der Flughafen Stuttgart, die Kunsthalle Mannheim, das BMW-Werk in Leipzig, der Potsdamer Platz in Berlin, der Flughafen Hannover, der Flughafen Zürich, der Kulturpalast Dresden, das BMW FIZ Future und das Innovation Center der Merck-Gruppe. Sibylle Schlaich und Heike Nehl lehren Informationsdesign und Typografie an verschiedenen Hochschulen und sind Autorinnen des Buches *Airport Wayfinding* (2021).

Sibylle Schlaich studied visual communication at Berlin University of the Arts and at HfG Schwäbisch Gmünd, Academy of Design. Heike Nehl studied visual communication at Bielefeld University of Applied Sciences. Together with Heidi Specker, Schlaich and Nehl founded Moniteurs Communication Design in 1994, a company focusing on information design and orientation systems. Moniteurs' most important projects include Munich Airport, Stuttgart Airport, Kunsthalle Mannheim, the BMW factory in Leipzig, the signage for Potsdamer Platz in Berlin, Hanover Airport, Zurich Airport, Kulturpalast Dresden, BMW's Research and Innovation Center (FIZ), and the Merck Innovation Center. Sibylle Schlaich and Heike Nehl teach information design and typography at various universities; they are also the authors of the book *Airport Wayfinding* (2021).

Projektdaten
Project Data

Bauherr Client
Flughafen Berlin-Schönefeld GmbH

Wettbewerb Competition
1998 – 1. Preis 1st prize, 2003 Aufhebung des Vergabeverfahrens und Neuauslobung als VOF-Verfahren, 2005 Beauftragung in 2003 cancellation of the award procedure, restart under the Contracts Procedure for Professional Services (VOF), commissioning in 2005

Entwurf Design
Meinhard von Gerkan und and Hubert Nienhoff mit with Hans Joachim Paap

Gesamtprojektleitung Overall Project Lead
Hans Joachim Paap

Projektleitung Project Lead
· Terminalhalle Terminal Hall
Martin Glass
· Ausbau Interior Fit-out
Petra Charlotte Kauschus
· Betriebsspezifische Gebäude Service Buildings
Rüdiger von Helmolt

Vertragsmanagement Contract Management
Jochen Köhn

Baumanagement Construction Management
Knut Nell

Mitarbeit Team
· Wettbewerb Competition
Sophie-Charlotte Altrock, Constanze Elges, Michèle Rüegg, Kristian Spencker
· Entwurfs- und Genehmigungsplanung Scheme and Application Design
Tomomi Arai, Sophie-Charlotte Altrock, Carsten Borucki, Constanze Elges, Ilja Gendelmann, Elke Glass, Martin Krebes, Bettina Kreuzheck, Helge Lezius, Birgit Ricke, Melany Schaer, Susan Türke, Christian Wenzel, Robert Essen, Ante Bagaric, Alberto Franco-Flores, Wido Weise
· Ausführungsplanung Detailed Design
Tomomi Arai, Ante Bagaric, Sabine Böttger, Lena Brögger, Constanze Elges, Sara Emrich, Chris Hättasch, Ivan Ivanov, Ursula Köper,

Bettina Kreuzheck, Johanna Kuntze, Helge Lezius, Ausias Lobatón, Doris Meyer, Anika Müller, Lisa Pfisterer, Susan Türke, Elke Glass, Kejwan Gross, Julian Hippert, Patrick Hoffmann, Irena Ludwig, Lucia Martinez, Thomas Neumann, Christiane Putschke-Tomm, Michael Scholz, Bettina Storch, Sara Taberner, René Wiegand, Achim Wollschläger
· Ausschreibung, Vergaben, Kosten
Tender Procedure, Awarding of Contracts, Costs
Stephan Both, Andreas Ebner
· Baumanagement Construction Management
Peter Autzen, Julius Hüpeden

Planungsgemeinschaft Flughafen Berlin Brandenburg Willy Brandt
Berlin Brandenburg Airport Willy Brandt Planning Consortium
gmp Generalplanungsgesellschaft mbH, Berlin
· Federführung Objektplanung Project Design Lead
gmp Generalplanungsgesellschaft mbH, Berlin
· Federführung Generalplanung Overall Design Lead
JSK International Architekten und Ingenieure mbH

Projektsteuerung Project Management
WSP-CBP Beratende Ingenieure GmbH, Berlin

Tragwerksplanung Structural Engineering
schlaich bergermann partner, Stuttgart
Schüßler-Plan Ingenieurgesellschaft mbH, Düsseldorf

Fassadenplanung Facade Planning
Prof. Michael Lange Ingenieurgesellschaft mbH Consulting Engineers, Hannover

Brandschutz Fire Protection
hhpberlin Ingenieure für Brandschutz GmbH, Berlin

Bauphysik Building Physics
Genest und Partner Ingenieurgesellschaft mbH, Berlin

Akustik Acoustics Engineering
Genest und Partner Ingenieurgesellschaft mbH, Berlin

Lichtplanung Lighting Design
Conceptlicht GmbH, Traunreut

Bildnachweis
Picture Credits

Leit- und Orientierungssystem
Guidance and Orientation System
Moniteurs Kommunikationsdesign, Berlin

Freiraumplanung Landscape Architecture
WES LandschaftsArchitektur, Berlin

Bauzeit Construction Period
2008–2020

BGF Terminal und Pier
GFA of Terminal and Pier
326 000 m²

BGF Bahnhof
GFA of Railway Station
25 000 m²

BGF Betriebsspezifische Gebäude
GFA of Service Buildings
35 000 m²

BGF Terminalnahes Parkhaus/Mietwagencenter
GFA of Parking Garage/Car Hire Center
130 000 m²

Davide Abbonacci
·   Seite Page 25

Marcus Bredt
Titelmotiv Cover
Bildstrecke Spreads
·   Seiten Pages 6–7, 48–52, 54–61, 64–86, 88, 90–92,
    93 (oben top), 94–98, 100 (oben top), 101, 110–111

Glanzlicht
·   Seite Page 23

gmp
·   Seiten Pages 22, 34–35, 36–37, 38–47, 53, 87, 89,
    93 (unten bottom), 99, 100 (unten bottom)

Heiner Leiska
·   Seiten Pages 20, 21
Skizze Sketch: Meinhard von Gerkan
·   Seite Page 16

Moniteurs Kommunikationsdesign
·   Seiten Pages 62–63

wibberenz'design – Hamburg
1   Modifizierte Welt- und Deutschlandkarte
    Modified world map and map of Germany
    http://d-maps.com
·   Seiten Pages 8–9
2   Modifizierte Karte Berlin – Stadtgebiet
    Modified map of Berlin—city area
    http://www.openstreetmap.org
·   Seite Page 11

Hinweis zu abgebildeten Kunstwerken
Information on the artworks shown in the images

Pae White: THE Magic Carpet, 2012,
37 × 27 m, Aluminium aluminum, I-SYS,
© Pae White
·   Seiten Pages 54–58, 62

Herausgeber Editors
Meinhard von Gerkan gmp
Hubert Nienhoff gmp
Hans Joachim Paap gmp

Koordination Editorial Direction
Detlef Jessen-Klingenberg gmp
Berit Liedtke gmp

Layoutkonzept und Satz Layout and Typesetting
wibberenz'design, Tom Wibberenz und
and Hendrik Sichler, Hamburg

Korrektorat Proofreading
Jutta Ziegler (d)
Tina Steiger (e)

Lektorat Editing
Detlef Jessen-Klingenberg gmp (d)
Berit Liedtke gmp (d)

Übersetzung Translation
Hartwin Busch

Bildredaktion Picture Editing
Sezen Dursun gmp
Berit Liedtke gmp

Reproduktion Reproduction
DZA Druckerei zu Altenburg GmbH

Druck und Bindung Print Production and Binding
DZA Druckerei zu Altenburg GmbH

Papier Paper
Arto Satin von by INAPA Deutschland
150 g/m²

Schrift Font
Linotype Avenir Next Pro

Bibliografische Information der Deutschen
Nationalbibliothek
Bibliographic information published by
the Deutsche Nationalbibliothek

Die Deutsche Nationalbibliothek verzeichnet
diese Publikation in der Deutschen Nationalbibliografie; detaillierte bibliografische Daten sind
im Internet über http://dnb.d-nb.de abrufbar.
The Deutsche Nationalbibliothek lists this
publication in the Deutsche Nationalbibliografie;
detailed bibliographic data are available on the
internet at http://dnb.d-nb.de.

jovis Verlag GmbH
Lützowstraße 33
10785 Berlin

www.jovis.de

jovis-Bücher sind weltweit im ausgewählten Buch-
handel erhältlich. Informationen zu unserem
internationalen Vertrieb erhalten Sie von Ihrem
Buchhändler oder unter www.jovis.de.
jovis books are available worldwide in select book-
stores. Please contact your nearest bookseller
or visit www.jovis.de for information concerning
your local distribution.

ISBN 978-3-86859-686-1